CHARACTER BUILDING IN KASHMIR

CHARACTER BUILDING IN KASHMIR

C.E. TYNDALE-BISCOE, M.A.

WITH FOREWORD BY

L T.-GEN. SIR ROBERT BADEN-POWELL

K. C. V. O., K. C. B.

GYAN

Published by

Gyan Publishing House
5, Ansari Road
Daryaganj, New Delhi-110002
Phone: 011-47034999, 9811692060
E-mail: books@gyanbooks.com

Distribution Network
gyanbooks.com
India, USA, Canada, UK, Australia, France

ISBN: 978-81-212-9310-5 (PB)
First Published, 1920

2nd Impression 2023

Printed at: Gyan Press, Delhi.

CHARACTER BUILDING IN KASHMIR

Author: C.E. TYNDALE-BISCOE

CHARACTER BUILDING IN KASHMIR

Frontispiece

Spearing Fish in the Dal Lake

CHARACTER BUILDING IN KASHMIR

BY THE REV.

C. E. TYNDALE-BISCOE, M.A.

HEADMASTER OF SRINAGAR BOYS' HIGH SCHOOL

WITH FOREWORD BY

LT.-GEN. SIR ROBERT BADEN-POWELL

K.C.V.O., K.C.B.

LONDON

CHURCH MISSIONARY SOCIETY

SALISBURY SQUARE, E.C.4

1920

FOREWORD

Mr Tyndale-Biscoe has succeeded in the delicate operation of strengthening the moral backbone of large numbers of boys in Kashmir, and in these pages he recounts in a fascinating way how this has been brought about. The book shows how, through Scout methods in capable hands, an effete race may be made manly, healthy, and Christian.

If this can be done in a far land with a foreign people, it gives boundless view of what might be possible and ought to be effected by the same means in our own great slum centres in England.

We are too prone to forget that charity has its greatest opportunity at home. Its greatest need is the men and women to carry it into effect, and the success achieved by the cheery author of this book should be a lever to move many to follow his great example.

ROBERT BADEN-POWELL

CONTENTS

LIST OF ILLUSTRATIONS

A WORD TO THE READER

IF you will look at the top left-hand corner on a map of India you will discover a country tucked away among the mountains, the abode of the everlasting snows. That country is Kashmir. It happens to be where three great countries meet—Russia, China, and British India.

Kashmir is one of the most beautiful countries of the world ; truly a land flowing with milk and honey. Pastures stretch for miles along the edge of the great pine forests which cover the mountain spurs, and here thousands of sheep and cattle graze. From these meadows, carpeted with flowers of every hue, the bees take the honey and hide it in the trunks of ancient trees.

One would imagine that such a country as this would breed a fine race of men, like the Afghans and Pathans on the border, but it is not so. True, the Kashmiris are strong and well built, but they have no pluck and no self-respect. The reason for this is not far to seek. In ancient days they were a fine race like the people around them, but their country being what it is — an earthly paradise — every marauder wanted it. So it has been conquered and reconquered by the Moguls, Afghans, and Sikhs, who have used the inhabitants as they desired and crushed all the spirit out of them.

Compared with the people of other parts of India, the Kashmiri is of fair complexion. Some have blue eyes and auburn hair. About ninety per cent. of the people are Mohammedans, converted to that faith by the sword. Except for a few Buddhists, the rest are Brahmans, the highest caste of Hindus. Until quite lately, only the Brahmans cared for education and attended schools.

Now, the Kashmiris are our fellow subjects; it is up to us to help them all we can to regain their ancient powers, to become self-respecting men once more, and to add to this that which alone can make them fit to meet their spiritual enemies—the power of Christ Jesus. If to know Christ is anything to us, it is our joy to pass on that knowledge.

C. E. TYNDALE-BISCOE

CHARACTER BUILDING IN KASHMIR

CHAPTER I

A PROPHECY WHICH CAME TRUE

IT was in the autumn of the year 1891 that His Excellency Lord Lansdowne came to Kashmir, and during a short stay found time to visit the mission school and speak to the boys. He spoke warmly of the work that the Rev. J. H. Knowles had accomplished in establishing the school amidst so many difficulties (one of them being that several of the boys had suffered imprisonment for attending), and to show his practical interest in this school he presented two medals, one of silver and one of bronze. These have ever since been the cause of friendly rivalry among the boys, which increases in keenness year by year.

The room in which Lord Lansdowne was speaking overhangs the Jhelum; as he looked out of the windows and his eyes fell upon the beautiful stretch of the river, he saw into the future, and expressed the hope that the State and the mission schools might ere long be competing in friendly contest for the headship of the Jhelum, as Oxford and Cambridge Universities strive yearly for the headship of the Thames.

Such thoughts were natural to a sporting English gentleman who had been trained from his youth in an atmosphere of manliness and fair play, but to the boys before him his words meant nothing, for that life of manliness and sports was as yet unknown to them. Was he not talking to holy Brahmans, the sons of holy Brahmans, who would never demean themselves and insult their godlike caste by doing boatman's work? Yet His Excellency was a prophet, and no false one, though his words waited for fulfilment for eighteen full years.

In order that you may in some way realize why the prophecy was so long in coming to pass, I must spin you a yarn, as it will show you the character of the Kashmir Brahman as he was twenty-nine years ago, and why it has been so hard a job to change the leopard's spots.

In the spring of 1891, about four months before Lord Lansdowne's visit, I was requested by the European community to take over charge of the boat club, and build them some rowing boats. As I had never built even a punt, I naturally declined the honour; but as they would not take "No" for an answer, and were so certain that I could build boats, I plucked up courage and undertook the job. A Frenchman most kindly came to my aid, and gave me the lines for the boats and found me carpenters, so that in a few weeks we had the required boats floating right side up on the Jhelum.

At the same time I built a boat for myself, and I remember that the paint for it cost more than the cedar wood of which it was built.

This boat was destined to play an important part in the training of the Kashmir boys, and especially of the Brahmans. I lost no time in sculling it down to the school in order to commence operations at once, as I, like Lord Lansdowne, had pictured in my mind's eye a racing eight-oared boat, swinging up and down the Jhelum before an admiring crowd. But I little knew of the battle that was awaiting me.

What a blessed thing it is that one does not know the future! Well, as I neared the school, the windows were crowded with straining necks and turbaned heads, all grinning and chattering, trying to force their way to the front, wondering what new folly this young *sahib* had taken to now. The sculls were put away, and so were the turbaned heads from the windows. School commenced, and soon all the students were greedily devouring the words before them (not necessarily the meaning) as they committed sentence after sentence to memory, swaying backwards and forwards as they squatted on the ground, droning over and over again the same few words, drawing in their breath through their lips, making a sucking, slobbering sort of noise. When the English period came, they were allowed to talk on the subject of boats, and I know that I learnt a great deal more about the Kashmir Brahman in that hour than they ever learnt about boats. But my learning in this line had only begun. These were some of the important things that I learnt during that hour:—

A Brahman must not touch an English oar, because on it is a button of leather. Although I informed them that there was no need for them to touch the leather button, moreover, that I should be angry with them if they did grasp the oar on that spot, they persisted in saying that nothing would induce them to touch an English oar or any other oar.

No Brahman must ever use a paddle or oar, or in any way propel a boat, as that would lower their caste to that of the despised boatmen.

This probably was the root of the whole business, namely, that the act of pulling an oar might produce muscle on the arms and, as muscle was only worn by coolies, my worthies might be mistaken for such low-caste beings. No Brahman had so vulgar an appendage as muscle on the arm.

Of course I informed them that, if they rowed properly, they would not get muscle on their arms, but on their backs and legs, and therefore their arms might still remain high-caste arms.

However, all argument failed, so what words could not effect something else should, could, and did.

Seeing the attitude that all the boys had taken up with regard to rowing, I determined to commence with the teachers, who would have more sense. I expected that they, being Brahmans, would be able to accomplish what I, as an Englishman, a man of no caste, was unable to do. So at the half-hour's "break" I asked two of the teachers to come with me in the boat, receive the first lesson in rowing, and so set an example to the boys. What was my astonishment when they also said that they could not possibly do so, using the same excuses as the boys had done. Well, here was a problem to be solved!

As a matter of fact, the solution worked itself out somehow, for in a few seconds, in fact before any one could object, the teachers, who a moment before had been standing at the top of the hall stairs, found themselves down at the bottom, and in a shorter time than it takes to write we were all on the river ghat together, looking at the bran new dinghy which was moored under the wall.

There was again a certain hesitation on the part of the teachers to move their bodies from the wall into the boat below, and so, for fear the spirit of argument might once again get possession of them, something happened which altered their position, and before they had time to think they found themselves sprawling at the bottom of the boat; I was in, too, and had cast off, and we three were quickly floating down stream towards the four-spanned bridge under which the water was rushing in swirls and eddies.

Now, in a boat one man must be captain and the captain must be obeyed; so I ordered my crew to grasp the oars, which they did with trepidation. I placed the oars in the rowlocks for them, made them sit on the seats, and ordered them to pull. As we were fast nearing the bridge broadside on, in order to save a catastrophe I had to take an oar till we were on the safe side of the bridge. But there were four more bridges below us. Those Brahman teachers had material backbones, if they were minus the moral article, and I had knuckles, so what with their backbones and my knuckles (I had placed myself behind them) and the fact that they were out of sight of the school windows, those teachers pulled their oars somehow. How we ever got back to the school ghat I do not remember, but we accomplished it. And we had done the up-stream journey by the prowess of two Brahman teachers, who had rowed in a boat with oars which had leather on them, and had made a beginning in making that low-caste stuff commonly called muscle!

That is history, and what Lord Lansdowne said was prophecy. What has been the result?

You will now be able to understand to a certain degree how the boys took the Viceroy's words concerning the grand sport of rowing and an inter-school boat race, words which were spoken about four months after this first introduction of the school to oars and their use. I need not waste your time with recounting what followed after that first trip in the boat, but suffice it to say that these two teachers were not the only ones who learnt to fly to the boat, and discover that they had backbones in two senses of the word.

If Lord Lansdowne could visit Kashmir again, he would see at the end of every summer the great race for the headship of the river, our ten mission

School Fleet on the Way through Srinagar

school boats finishing their race near the very spot where he had stood. But he would see something more. For the non-Christian schools of Srinagar copied us and, as long ago as September, 1909, felt themselves able to accept our challenge. The competing teams on that occasion, in addition to our own, represented the State, the Hindu, and the Islamia schools. That historic race, the first of many others, was rowed over a course of two miles, and our crew won by thirty lengths.

Then we were only at the beginning of things, since our eye was upon the goal, namely, that the work of the Kashmir boatmen might be considered an honourable employment, and that we might see crews of Brahman boys actually paddling with Kashmir paddles, not only using their prowess in racing, but taking out their families for change of air on the lakes, and in times of flood becoming life-saving boatmen.

I knew it would be a long fight, but had no idea that it would be such a hard one.

CHAPTER II

THEN AND NOW

TO my mind a school is an institution where citizens are made. When a new boy arrives we look at him, not in the light of a unit in the school—as to what he is going to do for its honour in examinations or on the playing fields—but one's eye travels farther; when that boy leaves the school eight or ten years hence, what sort of character will be stamped on that face? And in a day school, as distinct from a boarding institution, the life of the school must include the life in and towards the city in which the boy lives, which is the *greater* life of the school. The boy must be taught not only to think imperially, but to act imperially.

This being the case, you can understand possibly somewhat of my feelings when, twenty-nine years ago, I found myself for the first time in Srinagar—a huge rabbit-warren sort of place of 125,000 inhabitants. All streets crooked, all streets narrow, all streets filthy. The stench of the city had reached me long before I entered it.

One would have thought that the streets had been made with the idea of preventing any one from using them; for instead of cobbles, stones and rocks of all shapes and sizes had been thrown down indiscriminately, so that pedestrians had to pick their way from rock to rock, avoiding, if possible, the lakes of putrid filth that lay between. Not a single house in this city possessed sanitary arrangements. Had not dogs been created to feed on garbage? If one did not carry an umbrella, one stood a very good chance of a shower bath of slops down the neck from the upper windows; for street and drain were the same.

That which interested me most were the inhabitants of the streets, humans of various types and animals of various breeds. All were equally dirty, and all wished to keep the best of the filthy street for themselves. I learnt in a few minutes the position of women and children and the meek of the earth in Srinagar; for all who were weak had to give way to the strong, and all who were poor "kow-towed" to the rich.

The male sex pushed all women and children out of the path, but made way for cows and the pariah dogs, as the former have horns and the latter possess teeth. All this, and much more, showed me the lie of the land, and the need of a change, even in the unchangeable East. Now, if one desires to change or construct anything, it is usually wise to commence at the bottom. What better beginning could one desire than a school of young boys, and what better training ground could boys have than a city like Srinagar? When the two are introduced the one to the other, perfection is reached with regard to beginnings. So we encourage the boys to go out into the streets to practise what they have learnt in the school.

But the human material had first to be moulded into shape. I shall never, never forget my first sight of the boys in the school hall twenty-nine years ago. Some 200 dirty, evil-smelling human beings, squatting on the hall floor with mouths open, a vacant expression on their faces, and with fingers either messing with their faces, noses, or ears, or else holding firepots under their foul garments shaped like long night-gowns, the fumes from the charcoal and the heat of their bodies thickening the atmosphere of this low-ceilinged room. You can perhaps imagine the *froust*! As often as not the only clean part about the Brahman boys was the daub of red paint plastered from the forehead down the bridge of the nose, put on fresh every morning by the priest to show that they were worshippers of the god Siva. These creatures I was to call boys! "Jelly fish" was the only appropriate term to apply to them.

And I was to teach and preach Christianity daily to these. *Qui bono?*

What good could these be to their country? No! One's sense of smell cried loudly: "Scrub them!" One's common sense told one that it is as useless to preach to idiots as it is to preach temperance to those who are dead drunk. Help the idiot to become sane and the drunkard to regain his senses, and they will be in fit state to listen to reason. They must be awakened first.

Now, when I am depressed and have a fit of the blues, all I have to do is to look back twenty-nine years, and see once more those "jelly fish" who have since become self-respecting citizens, some of them leading the present generation of boys in those very sports which they once believed would defile their high caste. I think you will agree with me that talk would never have changed them, any more than the Galilee fishermen would have caught a multitude of fishes if they had not cast their nets as bidden, but only talked about it.

Christianity is a life that has to be lived. Christ Jesus was a perfect man as well as God, and to be a Christian one has to strive after perfect manliness —strength of body, strength of intellect, strength of soul—and to show that strength by practical sympathy for the weak. It is only those who are true men who can appreciate the Ideal Man. Some one has to create a desire for the ideal, and this cannot be done by talk, but by putting before the boys our great example, Christ Jesus, and asking them to join us in trying to follow that life, the life of service.

But how can a slacker and weakling desire such a life? They must be awakened first. I will ask you to look at the two pictures we can always turn up now.

Those rows of jelly fish squatting on the floor with heads on one side, jaws hanging loose, hands hanging listlessly down, saying they are of too high caste to row—that is one picture.

To-day you stand on the shore of the lake at the weekly regatta, and see the fleet at the starting post, the crews alert with all possible keenness for the word "Go," knowing that when the whistle blows a few seconds later, all the boats will have to disappear and turn turtle before they will be permitted to reach *terra firma* again. (This upsetting of the boats is most useful in teaching the boys coolness and resource in boating accidents.)

Again, look at those rows of high-caste boys who would not touch a man of another caste or religion—who, though filthy themselves, would never allow my hand to touch them for fear of defilement, and would squirm if by chance I patted them on the back.

Now see these high-caste Brahmans collecting at the boat-building yard (belonging to an old mission schoolboy who takes care of the school boats gratis) with the object of embarking in the boats which are going to take out the sick from the mission hospital or from the city.

In the former case they paddle for more than a mile through the lake and then walk 200 yards to the hospital, where the nurses help them to take the right patients. Those who are unable to walk soon find themselves riding on Brahmans from the hospital to the boats. Mohammedans on the backs of Brahmans! No wonder some of the Brahmans of the old school open their eyes at the sight and mutter mutterings.

For a long time the women patients held out

Embarkation Contest
The first boat afloat wins the prize

One of the School Boats and the Crew

against the boys' charms, but the boys have conquered at last, so that you will sometimes see women patients trusting their lives in the school boats.

The boys are always pleased when they have a full boat (the more the merrier) as they take their human cargo off to the open lake, singing as they paddle. The boys tell me that the women patients are not quite as easy to manage as the men, since they want to take over command, settle the course of the boat, and wish for longer trips than the boys approve of.

I have never met a boat crew returning with patients without the sound of vocal strains which they call singing; so one knows that it is a mutual pleasure. The landing stage is reached, and the patients are returned to the hospital as they were brought, and then the crews paddle back to the boat-building yard. Thence they make their way to their various homes in this great city of 125,000 people, having spent from three to five hours over their sick citizens.

How far the parents of the boys approve of this spending of the afternoons I do not know; they objected very much at first, but finding that the new order daily grows stronger they have had to put up with it, and are now beginning to see that there is some method in our madness.

Look again at the youth of Srinagar in 1890 as they stand in the hall before leaving for the classes, every one wearing a long, dirty night-gown of a garment, so covered with ink-spots and grease-marks (for it is used as towel, napkin, and handkerchief) that they look like so many bundles of rags waiting to be torn up into shreds at a paper-making factory.

Now this garment has almost entirely disappeared from the schools, and the more rational "patloon" (native trousers) and coat have taken its place. What attracts the attention is not a dirty night-gown but a small aluminium medal worn on the breast of the boys, on which is stamped the school crest and motto:[1] "IN ALL THINGS BE MEN." As some people do not quite approve of the motto for the mission school, let me explain what it means to the staff and the boys, whatever other sinister meaning it may appear to have to others.

I will first say what it does not mean by the following incident. A certain lady, visiting the schools many years ago, asked one of the little boys what was the meaning of his school motto, and he answered: "In all things we must not be women." This lady, knowing only too well the superior attitude taken by men towards women in this country, naturally did not think we had chosen a very gallant motto. As a matter of fact, we mean by men *true men*, i.e. those who combine kindness with strength. For we have all met the half-man specimen, the kind fools and the strong brutes. The perfect man is after the pattern of the Man Christ Jesus.

The paddles stand for hard work and strength.

The heart-shaped blade for kindness.

The paddles are crossed to signify self-sacrifice, and

[1] See title page.

remind us of the one great Sacrifice for all on that Cross of shame which is now an emblem of salvation, sacredness, and service.

This school badge means service. The boys understand that, if they wear this badge (they may wear black and red rosettes instead if they wish), they must be ready to render service to any one who calls upon them in difficulty and danger, as the people in England look to the police to help them. And I am glad to say that of late several boys have not been called upon in vain. This idea has quite taken on and adds much to their self-respect, since it is a badge of honour which must be lived up to. This service includes animals as well as humans.

Here is an opportunity for service. It has been pouring with rain for four days, and the melted snow comes tumbling down the ravines in the mountain sides, filling up the streams and rivers with debris. The rushing water has now reached the main river, and the news is telegraphed from Islamabad, forty-five miles up-stream, that a great flood will be upon Srinagar in a few hours.

This news naturally puts every one in motion; boats are hastily summoned, goods and chattels are removed from the houses to the boats, and all carriages and animals sent off in haste to the hills. The "bunds" along the river are patrolled by the officers, with gangs of coolies doing their utmost to strengthen the banks against the ever-increasing stream of flood water.

At last the climax is reached; man can do nothing

more, for the water has conquered, the many trickles have become streams, and the streams have swelled into sluices, the "bund" in all directions is crumbling and bulging and giving way—until with a great roar the river comes on tumbling over itself, wave upon wave, over gardens and meadows, filling up the lower storeys of the houses, until we are surrounded on all sides by a sea ten feet deep. Those who have been wise are on the hills or in boats. Those who have been unwise are up trees or on the roofs of the houses, calling loudly for help to the passing boats.

Among those who are unwise and calling for help is a party of sweepers, the lowest caste of the community. There stand several families, men, women, children, dogs, and hens, hustled together on the roofs of their mud dwellings, which are gradually crumbling away piece by piece into the flood. There are numbers of boats passing, but none will go to their help. Why? Because they are only sweepers, outcastes.

The women may tear their hair and weep, and the men cry aloud, but it does not bring boats. Fortunately for them one of the mission school boats, looking for jobs, happens to come their way and at once goes to their rescue. They can only take a few at a time, so they make several journeys, and thus rescue the whole lot of sweepers. As they take these low-caste people along, they meet many boats the inmates of which curse them for defiling their caste, but our fellows enjoy their curses and give them cheers instead. A boat in any flood is of value, but a boat with a crew above caste in a Kashmir flood is priceless.

It is chiefly in their service to animals that our lads come to grief, for the pony and donkey drivers resent interference with their property. The boys ask them to take the loads off their lame beasts of burden, and often follow up their unheeded requests by pitching the loads off themselves. This generally brings on a fight and, the men being stronger than the boys, the righteous perish and the wicked flourish as in days of old. But sometimes the noble art of self-defence brings the owner of that knowledge out on top. I know of one boy who got over the difficulty of engaging in battle (he was little of stature) by offering to carry a part of a lame donkey's load, and he and the donkey shared the load together.

Two boys came to their head master the other day in tears, sad to say, with torn garments and smarting skins on account of espousing a donkey's cause in the face of superior strength and numbers, and asked the master what they ought to do in such cases, "for," said they, "we are taught to succour animals in trouble, and when we do we are made to suffer for it." Action came first, and words second, for the head master, a Brahman and an exceptionally smart fellow, at once called for his strongest boys and started off in pursuit of the donkey drivers. But the raid was unsuccessful in so far as punishment was concerned, since the donkey men thought it wiser to trust to their legs than their sticks; they ran to cover, and left the donkeys and their loads to the boys.

The answer to the boys' question was twofold :—

1. That they should get on with their boxing, so that right might always conquer.

2. That all those who wish to put wrong right in this world must be ready to receive hard knocks and, if they are not ready to pay the price that every reformer has to pay, then they must leave the job to braver men.

Here we are in a great city with abuses of all sorts, shapes, and sizes around us. And here is the mission school of nearly 1500 boys and seventy-five teachers. What grand opportunities of service!

The jelly fish type has gone, not to live again, and young citizens are gradually coming into being, led by teachers who were once jelly fish, but have since grown backbones and muscle which are being used not in sports for sport's sake, but for the benefit of the city.

I look back twenty-nine years, and I see again those inane faces staring at me as I scull up to the school, and I hear the words of my European friends in those days as they said: "You had better leave this job alone, you will never do anything with this lot. Go back to England where there is so much work waiting to be done, and worth doing." Practically every European held the same view.

I now recall words spoken by a European last month. He said: "Do you think it wise to train up the Kashmir boys as you do, for these fellows

A "Splash-dash" from the School into the River

are a plucky lot; will they not use this power against us?"

We were standing on the lake side, watching the boys at their weekly regatta, swimming and boat races being keenly contested, and we had seen 107 swim across the lake, a distance of about three miles, only a few days before.

"Won't they use their power against us?" That is the question.

My experience of life is that brave men respect brave men, to whatever country they may belong. It is of cowards that we must beware, for they work in the dark as dung beetles and all sorts of creepy, crawling, slithery, slimy creatures do, whose words are softer than butter, but all the time having war and bombs in their hearts. No, friends, let us deal with men—men who can look you in the eye and respect you because they respect themselves. If these Kashmir boys become true men, strong as well as kind, what have we to fear, if we too are men? We will grasp their hands as brothers.

At present my fellows look at Christ Jesus as the most perfect Man, Who went about doing good, and they wish to walk after Him, and one's hope is that, walking after Him, they will find Him and, finding Him, will trust Him with their all as their Saviour and King, and go forth to fight for right, not only with the school shield on their breast, but under the banner of the Lord Jesus Christ. As the Viceroy's prophecy came true, so I prophesy that Kashmir will one day be won for Christ.

CHAPTER III

THE GENTLE ART OF CHEATING

WE are at cricket. I see a Kashmir sportsman walk round the wickets during an over, make some passes, and place something on the pitch in front of the block. To the uninitiated this means nothing, but to the batsman it means that the wicket has been bewitched, and the player, who is a Brahman boy, will be unable to keep the ball off his stumps. He stands before the bowler utterly unnerved, and becomes an easy prey to his adversary; he is bowled clean, and all those who planned the sorcery are jubilant.

We are at the inter-school athletic tournament. It is the hurdle race, run in heats; there are four competitors and four flights of hurdles. The umpire is just about to start the boys. I know that the umpire is not a sportsman, so I ask him if he has warned the boys about fouling, namely, that each boy must keep to his own flight of hurdles, and that if a boy fouls by taking another's hurdle, he will be disqualified. I stand by to hear the warning given. They start. The boy on the extreme right deliberately runs across No. 2, nearly tripping him up, takes his hurdle, and before he has finished has fouled another boy by taking his hurdle also.

There is another heat, and then comes the final. As I come to the starting point, I see the fouler ready to run in the finals. So I go to the starter and ask him why this boy is allowed to run in the final, reminding him of his deliberate fouling. "He did not foul any one," says this gentleman. I then ask him if that boy kept to his own line of hurdles or no. Did he run straight or crooked? Did he foul two boys or did he not? He answers that the boy did foul. Then I ask: "Why have you not disqualified him?" "Oh, it doesn't matter," says he. "But," I rejoin, "what order did you give to the boys before they started? Were they to run straight or crooked?" "Straight," he answers. "Well, did this boy run straight?" "No, he ran crooked." "Then I ask you, what did you say would happen to the boy who ran crooked and fouled?" He answers: "He should be disqualified." "Then have you disqualified him?" I ask.

By this time a crowd had come up and were trying to help the starter in his trouble. However, I fixed him with my eye, with the result that he told the boy to go away. I then turned round to speak to some one, when I heard: "Are you ready?" I turned to see the start, and there I see my friend the fouler in his place again, ready to start. I go to the starter once more and ask him why the fouler is there. "I thought you said that you had disqualified him." "No, I have not," said he. So I go through the same list of questions with him as at the first, he giving me the same answers and with the same result, the boy being told to go away. Again my eyes are attracted in another direction, when I am called to attention by the words: "Are you ready?" And then again for the third time I see my fouler friend with his toe on the line. The starter thought he had me this time, but he was mistaken. That boy did not run again in that hurdle race, and the starter, I believe, does not love me.

If difficulties stand in the path of builders of body, still more are there in the way of the builders of mind, and from quarters unexpected by those who know not the East as it is.

Examinations play a great part in the school life of boys in the West, but to a still greater degree do they influence the lives of the modern eastern scholar. The preparation for them is metaphorically his meat and drink, for so much depends on his passing them—government service, a wealthy wife, honour, the coveted letters B.A., and similar delights. As the time of an examination draws near, the students read for the greater part of the night, and use all manner of means for keeping themselves awake, even to tying their back tuft of hair to a nail in the wall. Examinations do not sound a very interesting subject, but in this country they can be most interesting, for examination passing has been worked up to a fine art, as the following incidents will show,

It is now many years ago that Kashmir was honoured by being made one of the centres of the Punjab University examinations, and I began almost at once to learn wisdom.

One of the boys, whom we happened to be sending up for one of these public examinations, had some time previously been reading in another school, and had for some reason, of which I am not aware, fallen foul of his teacher. This master wished to get the better of his former pupil by preventing him from passing and, to do so, arranged with the authorities to be made one of the assistant supervisors, when he would handle this boy's papers to his own advantage and the boy's disadvantage. Fortunately, I heard of this subtle plan a few days before the examination, and was able to send in another assistant supervisor who checkmated the man of arts.

At another examination one of my staff was sitting for his F.A. (First Arts examination), and his seat happened to be close to the supervisor's table, which proved to be his undoing; for a certain assistant supervisor, who was anxious that the would-be F.A. man should not pass, arranged to spin long yarns on interesting subjects with the supervisor, which made it impossible for my colleague to concentrate his attention. He complained several times, but without result. In this case the assistant supervisor was successful.

At this same examination was a young gentleman, the son of an important personage, who, although blessed with plenty of this world's goods, craved literary honours also. He, not having prepared himself by studying, provided a covered boat, roomy and comfortable, in which his tutor could sit and answer his questions correctly for him just outside the examination hall. The water-carrier, who came in and out of the hall to refresh the wearied and thirsty examinees, proved a ready means for taking the examination papers out and bringing back suitable answers. I would point out that it was winter time, when it would be difficult to work up a decent thirst.

I, in common with all mortals who have been to school and college examination halls, am quite aware that it is not always the deserving who pass. My memory carries me back to a school prize-day, the hall filled with parents and relatives of boys, who were watching with keenness and applauding the fortunate winners of prizes as they stepped on to the dais and received their rewards of virtue.

The boy who had come out top gave a knowing wink as he came back with his prize amid much applause. Many who were not "in the know" wondered, knowing that he was not a lover of book-learning ; but his class-mates knew how it was done, for he was proud of his wisdom, and had showed them daily before he entered the examination hall how well prepared he was. He had notes of his subject written most neatly in every part of his watch, and on suitable cards fastened with elastic to his shirt at the shoulder, which could be pulled down his sleeve, and would fly up at will when necessary; even his shirt cuffs were brought into use, which of course was risky.

Well, this boy won his prize by his own wisdom (of a kind) and was proud of it, not proud of his prize. He had succeeded in getting the better of supervisors of the examination. He looked upon it as sport, and he had won the game, and he thought that those who would not play this game were fools. There are always a certain number of boys in a school who look upon cribbing as this prize-winner did, but most of the boys in an English public school despise cribbing, and class it with all other forms of dishonesty.

It is not always the deserving who pass; when the undeserving succeed, it is by their own effort and trickery, and by getting the better of their pastors and masters. But in this country I was to learn that it is the pastors and masters who are past masters in the art of getting their own boys through a public examination when their knowledge of the subjects is deficient.

Some years ago I was requested by the university to superintend their public examinations here. I accepted, as I wished to discover how far it was possible to run an examination in this country in such a manner that the righteous might be rewarded and the wicked punished, even in this life.

The appointment was evidently not popular in certain quarters, for I was refused the hall in which the examination had been previously held, and was advised to hire the European hotel, which my adviser—great man that he was—knew to be out of the question. I was denied the needful quantity of furniture from the department which had supplied it hitherto; so that up to within three days of the event I had no idea what I should do, as it was winter and the examination could not be held out-of-doors. However, help came from an unexpected quarter, so that the day before the examination everything was ready for the seating of seventy candidates.

I had my own guards outside the hall to keep out all intruders (including water-carriers), as well as sufficient trusty men inside to circumvent young gentlemen wishing to get the better of their pastors and masters, and again two or three special men to supervise the assistant supervisors who had been sent to help (?) me. The presence of the latter I was obliged to have in the hall, but would have gladly dispensed with it.

Fifteen minutes before the hour appointed the doors were opened, and soon the hall was filled with wide-mouthed, jabbering, mannerless examinees, who no doubt thought that they were going to have it all their own way.

Just before the distribution of the papers I called out "Silence!" That had no effect. I then reminded the crowd that the time of their examination had commenced, and that no papers would be distributed until they were all silent. This remark also had no effect. So I sat down to read. Then gradually it began to dawn upon some of them that

I had the whip-hand, and they tried to persuade their friends to be quiet; and finally, after much valuable time had been wasted, there was dead silence, and the papers were given out. After reading through the question paper, many began to call out for various things, such as ink and paper, rapping on the desk, or stamping on the floor, and enjoying the noise they were making. They were then informed that their wants would receive no attention until they ceased stamping and rapping, and added the word "please." This remark seemed to amuse them immensely, and they continued the noise. Then when they realized that more valuable time was slipping away, and that no ink or paper was coming, they again came to the conclusion that obedience to orders was advisable. By the end of the week's examination all the examinees had learnt to obey at the word, to add "please" to their vocabulary, not to spit on the floor or make horrid noises in their throat, and various other little matters which add pleasantness to life.

The test was not so satisfactory from the examinees' point of view, for thirty-six out of the seventy were ploughed, and I was not popular in the city for some time to come.

One boy especially did not love me; I did not approve of his way of acquiring knowledge, for I always hold that knowledge should be inside and not outside, where it may wear off. This particular youth had covered his hands on both sides even to the finger tips with history notes written in green ink. He wore gloves like a gentleman, but I do not think that he behaved as a good Brahman, for he tried hard to suck all the green ink off both hands as he was walking from his desk to my table, which made a mess of his mouth. I should have thought green ink as defiling as the smack of a leather football in the mouth, but I do not pretend to be a professor in these matters.

One of the reasons given out by the city fathers for the failure of so many of their sons was this—that I had taken the papers to my house, and destroyed parts of the papers of those boys whom I wished to see ploughed. I thought this suggestion quite a good one even for Srinagar.

I will not trouble you with more than one instance of the joys of superintendence, of which I know not a few.

Soon after the commencement of an examination, one of the assistant supervisors came to me, asking permission to leave the hall as he had an appointment at the hospital. I pointed out to him that it was but 7.30 a.m., and that the hospital did not open until 10 a.m. However, he had his answer ready; the doctor would see him privately. I had been expecting this man and another to ask leave to quit the hall, and had prepared cycles and riders to follow them, as I wished to know which of the examinees they were so much interested in, and who were their confederates outside. I had been told that the suit of clothes this man was then wearing, and the cycle on which he rode, were both presents from grateful parents for his success in superintending former examinations. So he was a man worth knowing. Well, I allowed the poor, sick man to go to the doctor, but I did not allow him to enter the hall again, much to his chagrin. I also discovered who his confederates were.

About ten minutes after the first man had gone, the second assistant supervisor—who had been sent to help me in running the examination honestly—was also ill, for he had a pain in his "little Mary," which he pressed lovingly. I expressed my grief, and allowed him to go home as he so desired it. He was not aware that I had a cyclist also waiting for him. This man's "sickness" happened to be a gentleman in a house boat, who was greatly interested in a rich man's son in the examination hall. It is quite touching to discover what tender hearts some assistant supervisors have for rich men's sons, and I know quite a good few of such tender-hearted gentlemen in Srinagar.

When the results of the examination were out, one of the failed boys asked me to help him to recover from his priest a sum of money that he had given him. The priest had promised him success in the examination, if he paid him a certain sum of rupees and if he walked round the Fort hill forty times at night. There was not a sufficient number of nights to carry out the order completely, so the boy spent the valuable night hours before and during the examination week, stumbling over the rocks at night round the Fort situated on a hill outside the city.

Another boy came to ask my help in regaining

his property from a boy who had cheated him. This boy gave out to his friends that he had made friends with the devil (probably a fact), and that as a proof of his friendship the devil had shown him all the questions in the coming examination. His friends were of course very keen to share his knowledge, but he was very careful, and would only sell the questions one by one. In this way he had made a good business out of his Satanic friendship. When the examination was over, this boy was very much wanted, but he had left Srinagar for change of air with his assets.

Before any public examination, numbers of students go to the shrine of the goddess of music about ten miles from the city. So the priests in charge of this sacred place are very thankful to the Punjab University for having made Srinagar a centre for their examinations, and for encouraging the people in the pursuit of knowledge.

Before I came to this country I thought examinations most uninteresting, but here I find them full of interest and humour.

Hands in the printing works have a good opportunity of making money, as the relatives of examinees will pay large sums for an examination paper a few hours ahead of the examination. And the printers have more than one way of smuggling out the papers, one way being to sit on the type! When they resort to this expedient, some wear trousers, others do not.

But the superintendent has great opportunities for

rewarding the straight and punishing the crooked although the latter cannot be done in this country without making enemies. Is it worth it? I think so, for after all Rome was not built in a day.

It is worth a good deal to have a testimonial such as this translation of a vernacular letter, dated Srinagar, Kashmir, 1 April, 1908, from certain Hindu and Mohammedan inhabitants, to the "Members of the Mission Society":—

"PROTECTOR OF THE POOR,

"We, the inhabitants—Hindus and Mohammedans of Kashmir—respectfully beg to state that there is at the present moment a mission high school in Kashmir. Our boys attend the said school. But as long as there was Mr. ——, there was everything in perfect order, and our boys gained much learning and ability under him. But since the arrival of Mr. Biscoe, he has done nothing to improve the teaching of the boys, but has devoted himself soul and heart to all sorts of athletic entertainments and, above all, is attracting the boys towards his Christian religion, and notwithstanding the repeated warnings from the Maharajah Sahib, he has always given a deaf ear to all such. And it so happened once that he *forced* some Moslem boys to dine with him, quite against their wishes or religion, and made a compromise with the parents of the boys by bribing them, and now he is stretching forth his hands on Hindu boys, and the result is this, that 300 boys have been kept back from attending the school, and when asked to give them the discharge certificates, he did not give these and made a great fuss, and now all the students are wandering here and there. All these events are indeed earning a very bad reputation for the school and the Society, and a complaint has been made to the Maharajah, and a full and stern explanation has been asked, and we hope a copy of the same complaint has been forwarded to you. Now we want this, that if Mr. Biscoe is allowed to remain in Kashmir as a principal of the school, not a single boy will attend it, and the Society will have to close it for good, but if a man like Mr. ——, and an M.A., is put in his place, the school will flourish a good deal, and we all will do our utmost to help it in every way. Therefore, please, Sir, transfer Mr. Biscoe, for he is exceedingly a bad man, illiterate, deceitful, ill-mannered, uncultured, cunning, and man too much fond of cricket."

CHAPTER IV

THE BOYS TO THE RESCUE

IT was about eighteen years ago—I cannot remember the exact date, for so many struggles have taken place since that time—that Kashmir was visited by a very severe epidemic of cholera, which carried off its thousands of citizens, as it always does in unsanitary and filthy cities. Then upon this we were expecting a visitation of plague, as it had crept up India from Bombay very close to us, and was actually claiming its victims from Jummu, which is the second capital of Kashmir. So we thought that the time had arrived for the school to aid the doctors and municipality by waking up the city to its danger. Talking had long proved to be utterly useless. We in India are great talkers, and especially so in Kashmir. Action, and that prompt action, was the need of the hour, so volunteers for manual labour were called for. To our appeal over three hundred teachers and boys responded at once.

Our line of attack was as follows:—

Firstly, to ascertain the numbers of householders who were willing to receive a visit from volunteer "engineers," who would drain their front or back yards, and fill with river sand their private lakes of liquid filth. This canvassing revealed to us that seventy householders were ready for this "spring cleaning."

Our next duty was to approach the municipal officer, to inform him of the wishes of the seventy householders, and ask his help. This officer promised us his blessing, and with it he offered us the use of all the implements needed for the task, which included spades, shovels, and picks, with baskets and cargo boats for conveying the sand from the sand banks in the river to the death traps in the city. Having secured all the help we needed at the moment, we knocked off all school games for the more strenuous work of spade work.

We had arranged to start on Monday afternoon, teachers and boys wishing to commence operations as soon as possible. But when I arrived at the school that morning and was addressing the boys on the subject, I saw at once that something had gone wrong. Brightness on the faces of the boys had disappeared, the enthusiasm of the staff had given place to the hang-dog expression—to use a very expressive Indian word, they were utterly "gabrowed." So I could not forbear asking them if they all thought they were about to be hanged, which remark usually cheers them up. I did not realize that I had really hit the mark, for they explained to me that all those householders who had expressed their willingness for a visit from our engineer corps had changed their minds absolutely, and further, that the

Schoolboys at Road-making

Peace Day Celebrations

Dispensing Medicine during Cholera Epidemic

Carrying Logs for School Building

Brahman priests had heard of our intentions and had strictly forbidden any Brahman, whether teacher or boy, from undertaking this most unholy and degrading work, and threatening instant excommunication should they disobey.

The whole school looked at me for an answer, if any, to this Pontifical Bull. I must confess that it all came upon me as a thunderclap, as I had not prepared for this *non possumus.*

To show you how strong the Brahman priests are in their conservatism, one summer recently the municipality wished to clean up a most filthy alley and pave it with bricks. The priests, to prevent any such new-fangled innovation, lay down in this filthy fairway so that the reformers would have to remove their bodies, or pave the alley over them. The priests, of course, won the day, as no member of the municipality would dare touch the sacred Brahman bodies; so this alley remains to this day, as it always has been, a "Nehushtan."

It is this lot who try (and generally succeed) to block all reforms for the good of the city. It is these people who spend many days in the year on pilgrimages to the gods and goddesses who are supposed to live in the springs and caves in the mountains. Would that pilgrimages to those glorious snowy heights, and the entrancing beauty of the forests and streams, made them appreciate cleanliness and purity! But it is not so, for their eyes are still blinded and their hearts darkened.

What is the use of moralizing? We will get

back to hard facts, the struggle of years ago—the Pontifical Bull. I made answer to that Bull by telling my teachers to go and interview those holy men, and inform them that we were attacking filth and not religion, and therefore there was no need for their interference; but we would be glad of their co-operation in the matter of teaching the citizens how to save themselves from deadly visitations.

I am sorry to say that my words did not drive away the gloom, for they knew their priests better than I did. They went to their classes with sad countenances. I did not then fully realize how serious the matter was for them, and how tight a grip the priests had over their people, and I imagined that the morning gloom would blow off as the morning mist.

School was over at 3.30, when the boat containing all the digging tools was at the school steps. With the help of two boatmen I brought up several spades and picks opposite the school entrance, so that the boys could choose their weapon when they came out of school. No one dared come forward. I stood there for some time looking at them, with my coat off and a spade across my shoulder. The boys in the meantime were crowding at the door and windows, and I wondered how long this comic opera would continue. At last one plucky fellow stepped out and shouldered a pick, and then a second brave. We three stood in a row waiting for others to join us, but we were doomed to disappointment. For, all of a sudden, the boys raised a great shout, and came out at the rush, many of them covering their heads with their blankets (it was early spring), so that I should not be able to recognize them, and fled out of the school compound, passing us as if we had been lepers.

I was justly proud of the two who stood by my side—Brahmans, both of them. We proceeded to the boat which was to take us to our battlefield, which happened to be the compound belonging to the C.E.Z.M.S. dispensary. This the neighbours had used as a dumping ground.

As we passed under one of the seven cumbersome wooden bridges which span the river Jhelum (the Hydaspes of the Greeks), the crowd who had assembled on it to watch us hooted, whistled, and yelled at us as a Kashmir crowd know how. We three stood up and returned them three cheers, and before long we were out of range of their noise. We sped down stream in silence, doing a good deal of thinking, as we expected a warm reception when we landed; but contrary to our expectation we were unmolested, and walked through the streets with our tools to the dumping ground, which we intended to drain, clean, and turn into a garden.

As our march had been so peaceful we expected trouble at the dispensary compound, but we were wrong once more, for as we opened the door cautiously we found the place full of teachers and boys who had come by by-ways and alleys, away from the public gaze; they had come to help and not hinder. It is true that fear was written on their grinning countenances; nevertheless they had come determined to face the music, which soon began in earnest. We commenced at once to dig holes in which to bury the filth, sweepers being procured to put it into the holes so that the Brahmans should not defile themselves by shovelling it up.

The whole neighbourhood was on the buzz, the houses around were soon like a theatre—pit, galleries, and all the rest of it—a fitting frame for the sanitary comic opera which was being enacted, in this land of comic operas. All seats were taken, in windows, on walls and roofs, and every other place of vantage. The crowd in the dirty street outside the compound wall was packed tight with towns-folk who could not see anything; so they amused themselves by yelling and calling upon the volunteers to come away. But as these orders were unheeded, they threatened all the dire punishments that they could think of, some of which they really carried into effect later on.

Well, the boys stuck to their job until dark, and then melted to their homes in the same manner as they had come from the school.

The work continued day by day, nevertheless, until we had carried out our programme and made that desert place blossom as the rose, literally and not metaphorically, for we drained it, brought in turf, and planted flowers and rose trees. For some reason or other the neighbours ceased to defile the dispensary, which had been freely giving medical aid to their suffering mothers, wives, and children.

You can be quite certain that the opera did not

cease with the first act, for meetings both public and private were held in the city to condemn this unholy work, and efforts were made to bring trouble upon the school staff and to damage the schools, as you will see later on.

But there was one brave man in the city (there may have been more, but they kept out of our way in those days), the *tehsildar*, or chief magistrate of the city, and a Brahman to boot, an old greybeard, whose only son attended our school. This man came in all this hubbub to encourage me. He said: "In order to show the city that I am on your side, and that the tehsildar is not ashamed to use a spade, will you please give orders that my son shall always carry a spade across his shoulder when he rides home from school." So every day the towns-folk saw the strange sight of the tehsildar's son mounted on his smart little pony, sitting on a red and gold embroidered saddle-cloth, with a spade across his shoulder. Not content with this, the tehsildar borrowed tools from us, and he and his servants drained his own compound. Thus the holy city learned that their chief magistrate, who by caste was a Brahman, was not ashamed to dig.

But, on the other hand, the telegraph office was busy sending messages to the native press and to influential people, and among them Mrs. Annie Besant, of theosophical fame. Letters, no doubt of a very garbled nature, soon reached her, so that she felt it her duty to save the Brahmans of Srinagar.

Ere long she appeared on the scene and, with the

aid of certain native officials who should have known better, set to work to wreck the mission schools. They commenced by opening a rival school close to our high school, on the opposite side of the river. The next incident was a mutiny in our school, engineered by one of Mrs. Besant's disciples, which might have been a complete success had very prompt measures not been taken. As it was, three of the staff with three hundred boys left the school for the rival institution over the way, and became the nucleus of Mrs. Annie Besant's Hindu school.

The leader of this immortalized three hundred came to me about a week after the transfer, asking pardon and promising to bring back the same number of boys that he had taken away. I promised my forgiveness on the condition that he brought back the identical three hundred. This he said he could not do, so we parted. I knew we should get on without his help, and history proved that I was right; for in a few months our numbers rose from 500 to 800, our original total, and then went up to 1500.

Very many comic operas were staged in those days, which space forbids my mentioning, but there are two side shows in connexion with the original piece which are worth recording.

Many of the native papers had done us the honour of telling their readers what they thought of us, and gave accounts of what had not, as well as of what had, happened—chiefly the former. For many of the Indian papers greedily swallow the lies made

The C.M.S. School for Girls, Srinagar

One of the Brahman Lies Reproduced on Paper

red hot in Srinagar. One of the yarns that appeared is worth quoting :—

> "Mr. Biscoe, principal of the Church mission school in Srinagar, makes his Brahman boys drag dead dogs through the city."

This "spicy" bit of news took our fancy, and we thought it a pity that one of these yarns at least should not be founded upon something tangible, so we decided to help the editor of the paper in this matter.

We possessed an obedient dog, a spaniel, who was in the habit of "dying" for his friends when required to do so. The rest of the cast was quite easy—a party of boys, a rope, and a photographer. The obedient spaniel died, and remained dead while we tied a rope to his hind leg, and placed the boys in position on the rope for the photographer to snap.

So henceforward if ever we find a citizen disbelieving Srinagar yarns, especially those spun against the schools, we can produce this photograph to show that one at least of their stories is true. Papers may err, but cameras never (?).

About a year and a half after these days of digging, and "dragging dead dogs," I happened to be in a suburb of Srinagar where we had worked on a drain for some days, when an old white-bearded Brahman of noble birth (so the neighbours described him) fell upon my neck and wept. I fancied myself for the moment to be in Canaan in the days of the patriarchs. The cause of this tearful embrace was twofold, contrition for the past, and desire for my aid in the present and future; two tears out of every three went to the second cause, I think.

After wishing my old friend peace, I asked him why he had been lost to my sight for so long. He answered, still holding on to me: "When you and your boys were digging here for the good of the city, and men laughed at and cursed you, you thought that all the city was against you, but you were mistaken. I with others was watching you sympathetically, and praying for you, but we said nothing, for we were afraid. But to show you that I lie not, come and see what I have done to help you, how I have metalled the road that you and your boys drained. I have paid for it all myself, and now I need your help, for the neighbours are angry with me for having metalled this road for the public good, and are trying to get me into trouble with the authorities, saying that I intend to claim this road for my own. They lie, Sahib! Will you help me?"

I visited his road, which was a very good piece of work, and of special benefit to the women and old folk who used it daily on their way to and from the canal. He left me comforted, but wiping his tear-stained face with the end of the sheet he carried over his shoulders. A pocket-handkerchief in his case would have been useless.

CHAPTER V

A PEEP BEHIND THE SCENES

OWING to the peculiar circumstances of this country and the character of its people, we feel obliged to depart from the ordinary rules, regulations, and customs which are found in most schools and to adopt what seems to us best in this school in particular.

To commence with the assembling of the school—we have no bell, but we have a flag-staff; so up goes the school flag. Our school being situated on the river bank, and being a three-storied building, the flag can be seen from a great distance, both up and down stream. Our flag is an honourable one, for it has emblazoned on it the school crest and motto, which proclaims to the city our sentiments and meets the requirements of punctuality. Punctuality is not one of the virtues of the East, which considers it derogatory to high breeding. For hath it not the taste of haste about it? which is of course unseemly. Hence our determination that the boys of our school shall not follow the East in this particular respect. So we start our school day by being punctual, or at any rate we teach the boys that it hurts in several ways and various parts if they are not. I need not say that we did not teach this virtue in a day or without pain.

Roll call is a great opportunity for reading faces, spotting those who are ill in body or mind, discovering the reason, and then applying the remedy; also for ascertaining who are absent, and why. We possess a smart man with a thermometer, a most useful instrument, for most of the absentees are sick! This instrument is the very fiend to some absentees, though a godsend to others. Many of our students hate the man who invented this instrument almost as much as I did Mr. Euclid in my youth. Then it is as well to be the possessor of a sharp ear for voices, for some of the boys use theirs in an act of social service for their absentee pals.

We have a very useful board hanging on the school wall, on which is inscribed daily the really sick boys, their disease, the number of days of sickness, the doctor who treats them and, lastly, the name of the master who has visited them together with his report. From this board we learn much. In fact, we feel the pulse of the city. Sickness comes from various causes.

If it is sickness of body, the school doctor visits the sick boy in his own house, or he persuades the parents to send him to hospital. We have an up-to-date ambulance, presented to the school by English schoolboys.

It may be sickness caused by bad drainage, or want of drainage, which is more probable. If so, the matter is now represented to the municipality. Formerly we had to do the needful ourselves.

Possibly the cause may be poverty, or the sickness of the mother, which means lack of proper food. If this is so, the matter is reported to the secretary of the poor fund.

Or it may be sickness of mind, caused by evil persons in the city, of which class there are not a few. If this is the case, these scoundrels are sought out, brought to the school, and taught in a very practical manner that it hurts to molest or assault small boys.

Whatever the sickness is, we make it our business to search it out, and go to the root of the matter and stick to it until the wrong is righted, for we keep a dispensary of medicines that have to be swallowed by other methods than by opening the mouth. Through our practice of house visitation we learn much else besides the condition of the boys, and this knowledge is made use of for the betterment of the families concerned and of the city in general. It often means introducing the lady doctors to the houses, taking the members of the household to hospital, or calling upon the teachers or boys to render social service, which they perform in a hundred and one different ways.

After the opening of school, which comprises roll call, prayers, and the singing of a psalm or hymn of praise, and possibly a talk of two minutes or so on some relevant subject, the boys all double out of the hall to the tune of the band to their classrooms, where they line up before the form master for inspection as to their cleanliness in body and clothes.

This in the early days, now almost prehistoric, was

a truly Herculean task. One absolutely did not know where to commence with the cleansing. So we used to pick out the super-dirty ones, take them to the river ghat, and pitch them into the arms of father Jhelum, clothes and all. As in those days the boys were respectable gentlemen—they knew not the low-born art of swimming—a rope was fastened round the bundle so that it might live to be clean later on. This method was, I grant you, a trifle drastic for more reasons than one, but it had the desired effect: dirt became less fashionable.

The first stage in the education of cleanliness having proved satisfactory, we were able to proceed with the higher standard, which took the shape of teaching the use of the bath, carbolic soap, and the scrubbing brush. The scholars who were considered eligible for this higher course of study were deposited in a bath in the classroom (for we believe in object lessons) and scrubbed with the aforementioned brush and soap.

This course did not continue as long as the former one, as the pupils proved themselves apt learners. This was satisfactory, for it enabled us to proceed to the third standard, which is now a part of the school curriculum. It is more simple and very effective, and at the same time remunerative, not to the boy or the teachers, but to the school coffers. It is simply this: if the manager of the school detects a dirty boy after a teacher has passed him as clean, the teacher in question has to pay one rupee into the school coffers, in order to smarten up his eyesight in this matter.

The net result of this hounding out of dirt is comfort for those who dislike dirt, self-respect to the boys, and honour to the school. Clean clothes is a greater difficulty, for that matter is to a great extent in the hands of the parents, as they have to pay the washermen's bill, which seems to many an unnecessary expense. So we have appointed Friday as washing or *dhobi* day. We have instituted this custom in order that those boys whose parents are not *dhobi*-phile or, in plain English, lovers of washermen, may save their parents' pockets by washing their own clothes. Now a washerman's is considered a very low-down job, hence many boys are able to bring pressure on their parents, to avoid being chaffed by their fellow students. So, through this general dislike of the washing trade, we produce cleaner clothes on the persons of the students.

Roll call over, the thermometer having started on its hunt for the sick (?), and dirty boys having been dealt with, class work commences as in all well-ordered schools. The first period of thirty minutes is devoted to Scripture teaching. All the boys know that if they come to the mission school they study the Holy Bible. When boys express their wish to attend the mission school (in this country the *boys* generally choose for themselves to what school they will go), I always tell them what to expect—larger fees and fines than any other school in this country, compulsory games, which are unknown in the other schools, free use of the cane and other punishments, and that our Scriptures form part of the school studies. I have never found them object, but on the contrary they read the Scriptures keenly; many are the boys in whose hearts have been implanted a desire for righteousness and an admiration for the life of Jesus Christ. The life of Christ is unfolded to the boys with the aid of maps. We work by map so that towns and villages in that wonderful little country may be associated with kind deeds, with the hope that the boys may put into practice in their own country something, at least, of that life of service which was lived in Palestine, and still further that they may wish to follow in His steps and become His devoted followers and disciples.

Anyway, they learn that Christianity is a practical religion, that it has very much to do with everyday life and everything in life, and that it is quite a different business from their religion, to which they have been accustomed all their lives. They can see plainly the difference between Christianity, as taught in their school for practice outside in the city, and their own religion, which has produced the present conditions prevailing all around them. And again, they observe how many evil customs are changing under the practical teachings of the few on Christian lines. That life, lived in Palestine two thousand years ago, is bearing fruit in Kashmir to-day.

After the Scripture period come the classes for English, Urdu, Persian, Sanskrit, mathematics, history, and geography. Although cramming is not permitted and learning by heart discouraged, as these habits lead to deplorable results, we still hold our

Helter-skelter : School Cleared in Twenty-five Seconds

own with other schools in examinations. In 1917 our percentage of passes in the matriculation for the Punjab University examination was seventy-nine per cent, and the year before was higher than any of the schools in the State.

In the middle of the daily school course the gong booms forth for work to cease. Then the bugle sounds, which brings the boys out of school helter-skelter into the playground in twenty-five seconds; if they are longer about it than twenty-five seconds they have to go back and do the lightning descent over again, until their speed satisfies the man with the watch. Eight poles from the upper stories to the ground supplement the two staircases, and speed up the descent one hundred per cent. We do this in double quick time every day, in order to show our contempt for the supposed dignity of slow progression, and that time has its value. In other words, we just hustle the East.

The whole school is now formed up into one large squad, and goes through bodily exercises to the joyful noise of the band. After ten minutes of this drill the band ceases, and all the boys double off to their special apparatus, such as parallel and horizontal bars, horse, clubbing, boxing, skipping, high and broad and pole jump, rings, and trapeze. Then, when all is ready, the band strikes up and puts everything in motion at once, and you imagine yourself at Mr. Barnum's show. And once more you see a school in being.

This half-hour is, to my mind, the teachers'

opportunity for learning the true character of the boys. I am always sorry when other matters demand one's presence elsewhere. The boys are then just themselves, or if they are not one can detect it at once. One can see their virtues and vices, their strong and weak points, their likes and dislikes. Over some one grieves, whilst over others one rejoices. It is a perfect kaleidoscope of sensations.

Here a boy swaggers on the bars because he sees that he is being watched—there a boy is putting his whole soul into the business in hand. There is the instructor who allows a boy to shirk the trick on the horizontal bar because he funks it, for is not that particular boy the son of a friend of his, or some big man's son? Another teacher is wisely encouraging a timid boy to try the trick again. Now a boy is slacking with his clubs, there a small boy is taking really nasty whacks on his nose in good temper and playing up to his adversary. There, again, is the son of a *banya* (tradesman) funking from the gloves of an underfed boy who, notwithstanding, possesses grit that would do credit to that athletic fellow from the hills who is at this moment pounding a Punjabi. How one longs for one hundred eyes instead of a pair, in order to learn more in that all too short half-hour. Ah! there goes the gong; the revel ceases, and again the boys form up into their large squad, this time to pray for the King, the Viceroy, and the Maharajah.

Prayer ended, they stand to attention and salute the King-Emperor as the Union Jack is hoisted, and the band strikes up the National Anthem and afterwards the Maharajah's Anthem. It is while we are at attention, and in absolute silence, that we all remember that we all belong to the same great empire, and we thank God.

The band strikes up again, when all the boys double off single file to form a maze. We watch each boy as he passes, and learn more; for every boy runs and holds himself differently; some are painfully conscious, whilst others are as equally unconscious as they double past. Now comes "easy" for ten minutes, when both teachers and boys can take refreshments, if they wish it, before joining their classes. Some betake themselves to the illustrated papers which are fastened to the veranda walls in wire cages, where they can learn by pictures what is happening in the world outside. At the end of term there is an examination in modern history. Boys are not promoted unless they pass this examination. In order to encourage the teachers to take the same interest in the buzz of the world, a master's salary drops if his class fails to obtain the necessary percentage of marks in this examination. Nor does that salary alter until the class satisfies the examiner.

The Burmese gong again booms forth to call the boys from refreshment to labour, and all of them troop back to their classrooms for the second half of the school day.

I have alluded to the use to which we put illustrated papers. We believe in teaching through "eye-gate," and we make full use of picture postcards. Besides having books of them arranged as to countries and subjects for ordinary teaching, we have one set entirely for the British Empire, in order that teachers may have pictures of the towns of which they are speaking to pass round the class in our own patent hand frame. We have also assigned to most of the classrooms a country, and have made a dado of picture postcards composed of scenes of that particular country. The pictures are fixed in a long, glazed frame, so that they may be safe from dust, dirt, and marauders. Our hope is that, as boys remain in a class for a year, that particular country will soak into their brains as the maps on my classroom wall forty odd years ago soaked into my dull head. The small boys' classroom has naturally been provided with pictures of India; on the north wall, North India; on the south, South India; on the east, East India; on the west, West India; and round the central pillars, Central India.

Then in the kindergarten room, as we consider the boys too young to comprehend a country, we start them on animals grouped according to continents. Birds and butterflies have also their special places and, if we can find pictures of fish, they shall swim near the floor. The kindergarten room is already a regular Noah's Ark.

We have a classroom somewhat below ground level, devoted to submarines and any thing of a creepy-crawly nature. This room is where Sanskrit is taught, and those who patronize it are chiefly the sons of Brahman priests who still wear the old-fashioned dirty nightgown sort of garment and wooden clogs, and find it hard to give up the conceit and untruthfulness of their forefathers. So we place the Hun submarines down with them—let us hope with good results! Then, lastly, we have a classroom on the roof, called the Pigeon Loft, overlooking the city and the valley to the everlasting hills—a glorious view. In this exalted classroom we place pictures of air-ships and aeroplanes.

We have also started a geographical room and a historical room, i.e. we collect all maps, charts, and pictures we can lay hands on for the walls of those rooms, so that, when a class is being taught those particular subjects, the teacher and boys are in their element, and the instructor has helpful material at the top of his pointer. Six large wall maps show all our Lord's journeys up and down Palestine. Short notes are found against each town or village as to what our Lord did in them, thereby associating towns and villages with kind deeds, as in ordinary maps towns are noted for their manufactures, battles, etc. The mileage is noted from place to place, the mountains crossed, and the weary climbing up and down hill, which these boys know so well in this country. Further, they mark the great depressions of the Jordan valley, hundreds of feet below sea-level, with its tropical heat, and can sympathize with Him as they remember the oppressive heat here in the stuffy bazaars crowded with smelly people on a piping hot day. They can understand the attitude of the disciples entering Jericho after that hot march to the fords of Jordan, irritated by the persistent yelling of the blind beggar, and then shoving him away. We think we have found a way of making the life of our Lord a reality, and the Scriptures live again.

You must remember that, excepting a dozen Christians, most of the boys are Hindus and Mohammedans; hence we must make our Scripture lessons interesting and practical, or else leave the subject alone.

We have lately commenced making raised maps on glass, so that all rivers, lakes, and sea look like water and cannot be mistaken for dry land. I mention this because the boys, having no idea of what the sea is, cannot, of course, imagine its vastness. They thought that only the blue edging, as painted on maps, was the sea, and that the lighter colour must be land, and often they would write the names of towns on the sea. So now we hope that these maps will help them to grasp the fact that seas and rivers are two very different sizes of waters. Perhaps this instance will show you how difficult it is for the youth of this country to grasp anything which they have not seen, and to make them understand that which they and their forefathers have never known.

At different times I have sent thirteen teachers to see the sea and the greater world, in order to speed up things a bit. Hence once again (other people are also sometimes dense) the reason why we believe so strongly in teaching Christianity by deeds rather than by books and words, and why we lay so much stress on social service not being confined to teaching in class, but consisting in the practice of the sort of things which our Lord did Himself when He walked the bazaars and lived among men.

Every boy passes through the doctor's hands, so that we may know the insides of our boys as well as their outsides. We are also anxious that the boys should know something of their insides as well; so on the walls of the dispensary hang large coloured charts of the human body. To these pictures the attention of the boy is directed, so that he can see at once the exact spot where the trouble is, and learns further how to avoid that particular pain in future. This arrangement we consider rather more satisfactory than that of a boy showing his tongue, and in return being given a prescription to take to the dispensary. By our method sick boys become wiser than healthy ones, and their very troubles become blessings.

We have for many years run regattas and sports without rewards, and the result has been decidedly satisfactory, for the boys not only are not "on the make," but feel insulted when offered a tip for, as they tell you, "they have done the deed," whatever it may be, "for the honour of the school." Any one knowing the Kashmiri and his love for filthy lucre will appreciate this spirit.

I do not mean to say that this super-sporting spirit is yet very deep, but my belief is that, if we can teach the boys to love honour above rewards, we shall some day find an unselfish people.

CHAPTER VI

DOING OUR BIT

WE closed the year 1917 with an interesting and useful piece of social service, in which we simply had to follow and not to lead—quite a new experience, and a very pleasant one. Profiteers had been growing rich by cornering rice, which is the staple food of the people, and by charging their fellow-countrymen whatever they pleased. The butchers and bakers also thought that they should not lag behind; nor did they. But they counted without their host; for we happen to have a Governor (a Kashmiri by the way) fearless and of strong character, who at once grasped the situation, and acted promptly by fixing what he considered were fair prices for food stuffs. Then came the difficulty of seeing that his orders were carried out, for in some parts of the East it is one thing to make a law, and quite another to see that it is obeyed. So he struck out a new line by invoking the aid of humble but honestly interested citizens to act as a vigilance corps. This was composed of some twenty head-men from a carpet factory and fifty C.M.S. teachers. These seventy "Vigilants" willingly gave their work and spare time and their best services to help the weak against the strong, and to enforce obedience to State orders by systematically patrolling the entire city, and reporting to the Governor cases of rice hoarding, extortionate and unauthorized prices, and other malpractices. Many of the thwarted dealers closed their doors, and these had to be opened. Then it is a local custom for shopmen to have two sets of weights—the just weights being commendably placed on the shop front for all to see, and the false weights behind the counter for use. This and other such one-sided trade matters received due attention, and public approval; and this averting of famine prices and practical social service by willing Mohammedan and Hindu helpers still continues.

The Governor opened shops of his own, in which our men sold rice to the poor until the rice dealers came to reason. Our "V.C.s" had quite a busy time and many amusing experiences, for the poor blessed them while the dealers contrariwise dealt out curses. On one occasion a certain baker was overheard to say: "There go the fiends of hell, let loose upon our city by Padre Biscoe." Poor Srinagar!

Some of our men were sent up and down the river for many miles searching for boats of rice and fuel, which were hiding in quiet places while waiting for a rise of prices in the city. Others went into the villages to discover those who were hoarding rice, and also those who were smuggling it out of the country, as the law forbids the export of rice. They returned with interesting information which proved useful to the authorities. They also made themselves useful by selling the rice which the Governor collected, preserving order among the crowds of impatient townsfolk waiting to purchase grain, and seeing that the women and the poor folk were not "done down" by the strong and the rich.

It was a work requiring much tact and perseverance, and sometimes the use of muscles, for often women and weak persons were pushed into the river during the struggle for food, and a few were drowned.

The food profiteers on their part did not remain idle, for they had no intention of passively losing their chance of loot. They pulled the strings so successfully that our strong Governor was removed to another sphere, out of harm's way as far as the food profiteers were concerned, and we, his aiders and abettors, found ourselves not particularly popular in certain high circles. However, the wind changed again, and we found ourselves called upon to render the same assistance as we gladly rendered the winter before.

The situation was even worse than it had been in the previous year, notwithstanding the bumper harvest, the profiteers having increased in number and boldness. As the situation demanded promptness, we closed the schools so that all the staff might be able to throw themselves into the work. For we considered that feeding a city was more important than teaching boys.

Incidentally, this occupation gave us plenty of opportunities for social service, beyond the actual work of selling rice from 11 a.m. to 5 p.m. at thirty distributing places. We were able to show that we were no respecters of persons. When we saw a rich man come in gay clothing, we did not allow him to put the poor man or widow aside in order to be served first, or permit the strong to steal from the weak, which is often the case, as the following instance will show.

A certain poor widow had just been supplied with her dole of rice, when down came a rich man, who had been a judge in this city for twenty years or more and, although he had rich lands of his own, he seized this little lot of rice which the poor widow was taking home. I know this judge very well, as he has interested me as a dispenser of justice (?) for many years. The ways of men in this land are a wonderful commentary on all the books of our Bible, and especially the Psalms, proving over and over again that it is indeed a book of truth.

Our men had some amusing experiences also, for several people who wished to be served first, or to receive more than their share, thought that our men were out for bribes like the rest of their brethren. One of our men accepted the coin put into his hand, and then, holding it out to the crowd to show what a fortunate man he was, threw good money straight into the river. The crowd just opened their mouths! In this and many odd ways our men were able to show that the ways of men, even in Kashmir, are not always the same. We were very thankful to the State for giving us this opportunity of service.

Reference has already been made, in passing, to the alertness of our boys in preventing cruelty to animals —a besetting sin of the people of this land. Several times have I seen citizens throw boiling water on the pariah dogs which act as street scavengers. When these animals drop with disease and starvation they become food for the survivors. No one is permitted to put them out of their misery, as it is considered kinder to allow them to die a "natural death!"

Next to the dog-scavenger is the cow. Often have I seen these poor, starved creatures fighting with the dogs for the filth in the streets, and now, as a more modern drainage system is being extended, the dogs and useless cows find it harder to live in the winter. The extraordinary thing is that although the cow is considered by the Hindus to be a holy animal, and any one who kills one is put into prison for life, yet the Hindus will watch cows starving. As they pass them they will often touch them with a garment and then put the garment to their lips, so that the holiness of the cow may in some way benefit them; but they will see a cow drop down from exhaustion, the carrion birds pecking at it while life still remains, the poor beast trying to shake the birds off—they will see its terrible death, yet will not move a finger to save or protect it.

This is an attitude it is impossible to understand, but I am determined that the boys who come under the Christian influence in the schools *shall* understand it, *shall* perceive the shame to their religion, *shall* realize the hollowness of their cow holiness, and *shall* see the insult to Almighty God, Who has committed to the care of men cows as well as other animals. Since those days the boys have been learning, and are continually putting their new-found faith into practice.

And next to the cow, in the matter of ill-treatment, comes the horse. One or two of our boys found a horse with a broken leg lying in the bed of a river. It had been one of a pair bringing a landau into the city. Its partner was restive and broke its leg with a kick. The driver unharnessed the poor animal, dragged it off the road and down into the river, to be out of sight and out of mind, hoping that it would soon die, and be hidden from view for ever in the stomachs of the pariah dogs and birds of prey.

Our boys did not think that this way of looking at things was quite satisfactory, so they went off to the city and brought food for it, and then came to me for advice. It was then 9 p.m. I am unable to write what happened next, but on the following day when the judges arrived and the court sat and gave its decision on this case, it became lawful to put the poor beast out of its misery, and it was shot accordingly. The cruel scoundrel, who was fined by the court ten rupees, was very angry with the boy who informed against him, and threatened to burn his house down. Since then scores of men have been convicted, so that from 300 to 350 rupees are paid into the court as fines every month.

On another occasion one of our boys found a donkey with a sore back and lame, so he made the man remove the load from the donkey on to his (the driver's) back. It is very seldom now that one sees an ill-used pack animal in the city, and we receive only about half a dozen starved and wounded animals annually, owing to the passing of a law directed against their ill-treatment. To our boys belong the honour of being the first to put this law into action.

With regard to kind actions on the part of our boys towards human beings, it is a little difficult to select examples, since most of those on behalf of women consist in carrying their loads, cutting up firewood, and such-like. During the year 1918 two stand out in my mind, since they justify the teaching of the noble art of self-defence.

A woman had been enticed into a house, and was about to be assaulted by a Mohammedan *pir* (saint), when one of our boys happened to hear her screams and, although himself a Mohammedan, feared not the "saint" but called men to the rescue and saved her.

Then, on another occasion our boys fell in with a party of hooligans who were beating a woman, and ran to her help. A free fight ensued in which our boys came out victorious, but with loss to themselves in the matter of property.

A matter which is worrying my men just now is the shameful custom of early marriage. It has been brought to our notice lately that several little girls have died in childbirth. If the wrong had not been sanctioned by marriage, these murderers (for what else are they?) would presumably be in prison, with deserved sentences of several years. A short time ago we heard of a girl, aged 12 years, being married to a man of 26. So my men went to him, expressed their opinions plainly and forcibly, and extracted a promise that he would leave the girl with her mother until she was old enough to bear a child without danger. Now we hear that the scoundrel has broken his promise, and taken the girl to his house; he has public opinion on his side and we are considered to be meddlers.

In order to stop early marriage we charge double fees to any boy who marries before the age of 18. Last week I was begging a certain leader of the city to do what he could to alter this shameful state of things. He told me that he was doing so, that he had held a meeting of the leading Hindus in the city, and that they had promised to try to prevent girls being married before the age of 13; in fact, he said, their leader was just going to marry his daughter of 13, which he considered was a good example to the city!

The blind, like the poor, are always with us, smallpox being one of the great causes of total blindness, as few people escape. A few years ago I took a census of the boys in the schools, and I discovered that out of the thousand boys only one per cent had escaped this fell disease, and that those few had all been vaccinated. Although blind men are usually very clever at finding their way about without help, some nevertheless get into difficulties and lose themselves, or fall into drains, etc.; hence the boys find opportunities of service in this line.

Our staff add nursing to their other duties when epidemics visit us. Look at this scene. We are in an upstair room in a house in the city, full of relatives who have come to mourn and groan by way of sympathy, and to see the last of their friend. He is one of my teachers, in the last stage of cholera; his fellow-teachers, with their coats off, are massaging his arms and legs to relieve him of the terrible pain of cramps which is upon him; the teachers have arranged themselves in watches of two hours' duty, all through the night.

I had just given him a teaspoonful of brandy, when the man who was holding his head said to me in a whisper: "Please, Sahib, leave the room." Thinking that it was on account of Hindu women present, I did so. Early next morning the man came to tell me that the teacher was dead. I asked the time of his death. He answered: "Directly you put the brandy in his mouth he passed away, but I did not tell any one of the relatives for fear that they would say that you had killed him; also on account of the women, for women hear bad news better in the morning than at night. We massaged his limbs so that those in the room might not know that he was dead till the sun rose."

There were these teachers massaging a cholera corpse all night! They knew well the risk they ran of infection, but they stuck to it in order to save me, and lessen the shock for the female relatives.

The following list of kind deeds was brought to my notice during the year 1918:—

Lives saved from drowning . .	19
Help given to women . . .	92
„ „ children . .	60
„ „ old men . .	23
„ „ blind folk . .	17
„ „ neighbours . .	60
„ „ animals . .	15

Work, done by parties of boys, included help given at eleven fires; the school band gave six entertainments at hospitals, besides playing through the city on joyful occasions; boys in squads lent their muscles thirty-two times; others lent their brains in teaching in a night school for several months; crews of boys took out patients from the hospitals and city, making fifty-six trips and carrying over three hundred sick folk.

And, of course, boys make use of their boating knowledge by recovering boats that get loose and wander down stream. The ordinary citizen sits and watches the boat float away out of sight, and amuses himself by wondering where it will fetch up. Our boys also go to the help of boatmen towing up their barges against the heavy stream under the arches of the bridges. I wonder if the boatmen ever ask themselves why the mission school boys bother themselves about them and their boats, for no one does anything in this country without a view to the main chance. Are these boys paid for it? If not, what fools they must be!

* * * * * *

"To Padre Biscoe Sahib Bahadur (the treasure of kindness), Protector of the Poor, may you be in peace:

"With hundred respects, I beg to state at 1.15 a.m. there broke out a great fire near my house, on account of which all my neighbours were in great consternation. In the meantime Pandit Samsar Chandji, who is a master on your staff, climbed over the wall, and with great sympathy and bravery supplied water, with other helpers, and put down the fire.

"I pray for the British Government from the core of my heart, who have sent Padre Sahib who infuses such noble, practical education, has created thoughts of helping and of kindness in masters and boys; for this I thank Padre Sahib from the bottom of my heart."

My readers may draw the conclusion from the above letter that every one loves me from the core of their hearts; so in order that they may understand that there are just a few who object, I quote the following letter, written when I was on a visit to India:—

"We know that devil Biscue. . . . Warn him that if he puts foot into our sacred Kashmir he would be driven out bare foot in his shirt, and would be drawn with wild horses."

N.B.—Perhaps the writer meant asses!

CHAPTER VII

THE CHARACTER SHEET

THAT Kashmir boys should notice cruelty, that they should wish to see things altered, and that they should be willing to suffer in order that they may save suffering—facts like these show that a new spirit is abroad.

Where did these ideas and their practical enforcement come from? From Hinduism and Mohammedanism? If so, why have they waited all these years till Christ's life has been preached to them? No, you who read this know that it is through the power of Christ's example when on earth, and by the power of His death and resurrection that the true light has come into this world. And, if the East is to know of this light, it must come again through the East as it originally came from the East. We Westerners can only show the way, and start the nobler spirits of the nation in leading the van. Each nation must have its own knight errants. Hence our school is not a factory for turning out passed or failed examinees, as are so many schools in India; nor is it a temple of learning in the ordinary sense, though we have the same curriculum as the ordinary high school, and have no reason to hang our heads because of any failure to carry off academical honours; but it is a workshop for building *men*, notwithstanding our failures, which are very many.

The character sheet (see last page) will show you at once our somewhat comprehensive scheme of training.

I will not describe it; I will only remind you that this report is filled up three times a year for each boy. That it entails a great amount of time and labour goes without saying, but my staff and I do not grudge this in the least, as every year shows more and more its usefulness in enabling us to know each boy, and therefore to help him; it also makes the teachers character readers, which is all important.

To give you an idea how faithfully our teachers watch their charges and do their work of "foster father," which is by no means a sinecure, I will pass on to you the conversation which took place between me and one of my staff who was bringing before me the members of his own class one by one in order to pass them through their character sheet for the term just ended.

Case I.—A tall and very serious looking youth has just been before me, and on his departure I ask why he has been given such high marks for "citizenship," as he did not give one the impression of being very energetic. The master answers that his looks belie him; he has a very kind disposition, for he is in the habit of going off by himself and hiring a boat on the quiet and taking sick neighbours out on the lake for fresh air and change.

Case 2.—An athletic, strong fellow, a member of the school cricket team, with hard and insolent looking eyes. I say to the master that I do not like the look of those eyes. I see that they are not so unpleasant as they used to be, but why is it that this look dies so hard? I am told that is not altogether this boy's fault. "It is this way, Sahib, (waxing vehement)—his father, brothers, and cousins are all in the Forest Department, and they have plenty of opportunities of looting the villagers and they do not neglect their opportunities. He is much better than they, but it is hard for him not to follow their lead."

Case 3.—A boy with a hunted-hare look now stands in front of me. What is the cause of this? I ask. Answer: he has not a happy home, for he has lost both his parents, and his step-mother with whom he lives has not a very agreeable temper; hence the result.

Case 4.—A boy with very cheeky, deceitful eyes. On asking the reason, I am told to look at the trade of his father, and that will explain. I look, and note that his father is a money lender.

Case 5.—"You have given this boy very high marks for citizenship." "Yes, for he deserves every one of them. He is a rich man's son, and is always doing kind actions towards his neighbours, helping the sick folk and the old women." This boy the other day was brought before me for some fault, and when I had finished the jubation, he stammered out something which fairly amazed me, for I had never had such a request made before. It was that I should give him a beating, so that the evil might depart from him! He was in dead earnest. I am afraid my heart was hard, and I refused his request, telling him to go and do his best to undo the evil he had done.

Then by the sheet I see what my staff of seventy men are doing or not doing, as the case may be. It is by this method that I am able to keep in touch with the hundreds of boys, who thus become individuals and not units. The sheet has taught me more about the boys, their families, and their environment in the city, than I could possibly have learnt in any other way.

I will pass on to you just three curious incidents that came out through the character sheet one year.

A little Mohammedan boy is brought to me, and I see that the character sheet and his appearance agree. He is in a weak physical condition, and an inquiry elicits the following story. His father has been hard up of late owing to the money he has spent in long journeyings, and therefore his family have been more or less starving. What was the reason of this travelling? His elder brother, a boy of above 12 years, was kidnapped by a woman while he was playing in the bazaar, and she sold him to some men going to the Punjab. When the father found out where his son had gone, he set out to search for him in the towns of the Punjab, and after weary travelling found him in Sindh, married to a rajah's daughter.

You would have thought that the father would have returned a rich man to live in peace and plenty for ever afterwards. But we are in the East, where many things are upside down. As the rajah did not do his duty, we set to work at once to do part of it by feeding the boy out of the schoolboys' poor fund.

A bright Brahman boy stands before me, strong in body and lithe of limb. I see that he has got very high marks for *esprit de corps*, and ask the tutor why. He answers: "This boy is a splendid chap; he always disobeys his father, and therefore I have given him high marks." On my raising my eye-brows, the tutor continues: "This boy has a fool of a father, who forbids his son to join in any of the school games; but the boy always disobeys him, turns up regularly, plays keenly, takes part in the weekly regatta, and so gains marks for his school." (The six schools are always engaged in continual contest as to work, games, making money for the poor, etc.)

A poor frightened-looking little boy faces me. I see at once that it is a case of home treatment (generally a step-mother).

"Whose son is this little fellow?" I ask.

"The son of ——," says the tutor.

"But how in the name of fortune did that man send his son to us?"

"Because he said that it was the safest place to which he could send his son."

I must confess I felt honoured. The father of

this boy is the soundest scoundrel unhung. Oh, what a hunt he gave us! And what a successful hunt it was! To make a long story short, this man, an ex-police officer, selected one of his quarries, an old schoolboy, and, after annexing most of his money, had him run into the *criminal* gaol for debt. There I found the young fellow in a pitiable condition, for, although a Brahman, he had not been allowed to wash all the time he was in gaol, and the gaoler had taken care that he should not over-feed. We took the matter up, and the judge apologized for a miscarriage of justice, and had the boy removed to the *civil* gaol. While the scoundrel's quarry was out of the way under lock and key, he sent round men of his own kidney to molest the unprotected women in the prisoner's home. This of course brought our scouts into play, those being selected who were handy with their knuckles, and they protected the women, day and night.

When the boy had served his term, the same rascal was at him again, and would, no doubt, have placed him again in durance vile had we not managed to help him to escape. He carried on his business from Simla, the school scouts aiding him.

These character forms are an unending source of interest, leading both directly and indirectly to practical work. It is this knowledge of things as they really are in this city of 125,000 inhabitants which gives us the opportunity of social service, for it takes us right behind the scenes, into the homes, behind the purdah, into the temples, and into the dark as well as the bright corners of the city and Srinagar society.

If the reader will look at the top of the character sheet he will note that we chronicle, under the words "Probable Loot," what a parent is worth in the market of honour and dishonour. I am afraid it shocked a certain rich *babu* (English-speaking clerk) to read such words. He said he wondered how a man who considered himself an educationist could give away the fathers of his boys in that unseemly manner, as it would teach the boys to despise their parents. I, on my part, certainly was surprised at a rich babu imagining that a boy of this country would be ignorant of this universal method of acquiring wealth.

This matter of "loot," or dishonest gain, is one of the chief temptations for which we try to prepare our boys. For in this country *dishonesty* is the best policy, and it beats me to think how any boy is going to stand up against it unless he possesses the strength that cometh from God alone.

Let me give one instance of more than probable loot.

Here is the father of one of my students. His pay is twenty rupees per month as a clerk in a certain office. His office is thirty-three miles from Srinagar, so he is obliged to keep two establishments going, his own and that of his family in Srinagar. His own living would cost nearly the whole twenty rupees, since he, being a Brahman, has to keep his own Brahman cook, who has to be paid and fed. Then his family in Srinagar could not possibly live on less than the twenty rupees, for every member must be fed and clothed, and the school fees and books of the schoolboys paid for. But, beyond all this, he keeps two clerks to help him to do his work, and he pays each of them Rs 7-8. These two clerks in their turn cannot live on that pay, for they have their families to support. And so the ball rolls on!

Now, any boy who is not an absolute idiot must know that his father cannot possibly be living on his pay, and furthermore, he jolly well knows that he does not, and thinks what a 'cute dad he possesses! We reckon that men in State employ make from double to four times their pay, according to their opportunities and acuteness. This will show you that there is no mean fight before these boys, if they intend to walk in the way not trodden by their forefathers. There is, of course, a difference between offices and offices, and departments and departments, in proportion to the character of the man at the head.

This is a subject that is of vital importance to us who are preparing boys for the battle of life. We have to know much about the state of the loot market, and not to talk about it too much, otherwise we shall get ourselves disliked in certain high places.

Anyway, whether we like it or not, we have not to take things as they are, and make the best of them, but to peg away in the firm belief that, with the help of God, our C.M.S. school will one day smash this loot market, and other similar evils that defile the fair land of Kashmir, and make up an army of honest citizens, ready and prepared for the day of battle.

CHAPTER VIII

YARNS ABOUT THIS AND THAT

A Put-up Job

AMONG the events at one of our school regattas was an incident which aroused a considerable amount of interest. A party of cleanly-dressed Kashmiris, presumably come from the city to see the regatta, was upset; to which there hangs a tale worthy to relate. A certain Brahman master was put in charge of this last item on the programme. He had received orders to see that this boat-load started from the bank round the corner up to time, and was generally responsible. This crew of ladies and gentlemen put off, and came down the course jabbering and chatting about rupees and rice, according to universal custom. To the horror of all who were not in the know of the thing, the boat was capsized in twelve feet of water. Amid the shouting and spluttering and splashing, and supposed-to-be drowning, was the Brahman master in charge, being held up by some of the actors, until saved by the reserve boat. On his return to the shore he was asked what made him enter the boat that was to be upset, knowing that he could not swim. His answer was: "Because the Sahib had put this event under my charge, and I could not have carried out his orders satisfactorily without being present myself at the upset." Are not the leopard's spots changing?

A Pretty Severe Test

On one occasion we started in rain and heavy wind to go by boat to Bandipore, seven miles distant. We soon had our jiggermast smashed in half and our mainsail blown away, but we still held on our course with our twelve oars. When within about two miles of our destination, we stuck on the shallows and, not knowing the navigation of those parts, had half an hour's uninteresting punting in soaking rain as we tried to find the channel. However, we kept up our spirits with the thought of hot tea and cakes in Bandipore, and as soon as we got ashore made tracks for the shops. But alas! the holy Brahmans of Bandipore swore by all the gods they knew (and they know a good many) that there was no Hindu food in the place. It was useless to ask them how they lived, etc., for some reason, best known to themselves, they would not supply any.

There were plenty of Mohammedan shops, but the boys, being chiefly Hindus, could not on account of their insane laws touch any food from there. So they made their way back to the boats, cold, soaked to their skins, tired, and hungry. They had had no food for several hours, but were in no way out of spirits, and still jolly. I said to them: "What is the good of your being hungry when there is plenty

The Wular Lake, Kashmir

of food around you. You cannot think that God made such a foolish law?" They answered: "Our law-giver evidently was not a traveller, but had his meals regularly, and therefore made no provision for hungry travellers."

We were soon in the boat and ready to start back on our seven-mile row through a stiff breeze, which anon worked up into a gale. The boatmen on the shore implored us not to go, saying that we should most certainly all be drowned; and this they thoroughly believed next morning, when one of our broken oars was washed ashore. News was sent up to Srinagar that we had all perished, much to the consternation of the boys' parents.

Only one boy showed signs of fear. He said: "I don't mind being drowned myself, but I have a little brother at home whom I love very much, and he would grieve so much for me." It was quite dark before we reached our camp, and we were met by a crew of boatmen who had put off from the village to search for us and pick up the pieces. A grand time we had of it.

How to Understand a Man

I do not think that a chief's duty is over when he has paid his men their salaries. Our work is not done for so many rupees, as is the case with a coolie, but is the work of a friend for a friend; still more is it a labour of love, a work of constant service for their fellow-countrymen. Some years ago it was no uncommon sight to see one of the staff standing before me with hands clasped in the attitude of prayer, with his head on one side, and possibly the toes of one foot scratching the other bare leg, asking for a favour. The sight was a sickening one. A so-called man, standing like a slave before a slave-driver! Those days are gone.

The slave chains were not struck off with one blow; it was a matter of years. Various methods were tried—constant intercourse out of school; going trips together on the mountains or on the lakes, where we shared fatigue, and more than once passed nights without sleep, hungry because our food coolie had bolted for fear of ghosts and hobgoblins on the mountains; many upsets in river and lakes; and once and again in danger in fires in the city, and in squalls on the lakes when sailing. For it has been a tradition with us—a very foolish one, no doubt—not to take in a reef, but to trust to the shifting ballast of a dozen or so of the crew on the windward gunwale. These are the times when we get to understand one another's peculiarities.

Breaking down Serfdom

Formerly at meetings of the staff the masters all sat round and listened to their chief, and everything that he said was "very good, quite right, could not be better." I was an amir, and my subjects faithful slaves. But gradually things have changed, and now, if you were to attend one of our Sunday afternoon meetings, when we sit in the garden and talk over matters to help us in our moral and spiritual life, you would see at once our position. Or come to our week-day meeting, at which we discuss the week's work and the social problems of this large city, and you will see that we are a parliament and not an absolute monarchy. Every one is encouraged to speak out his mind fearlessly, and I am able to state that, so far, not one of my own lot have ever presumed on this freedom.

It is the custom in this country, when men of different standing go out together, that they never walk side by side, but one just a pace or so behind the other. It is a most amusing sight to see a lot of clerks leave office together. The head babu stalks on in front, then comes the second clerk a few inches behind him, and then the third, and so on, each one wishing to get up to the front, but not daring to do so. That is how my staff used to try to treat me. I should by rights walk in front with my lower chest well to the fore, head erect, and at a respectable pace (two miles an hour), throwing my words behind me to my faithful followers tailing off in the rear. But now they understand my peculiarities and walk by my side, in front, or anywhere.

A Reason for Fidgeting

We have to work from the top and from the bottom at the same time, making the masters into comrades and developing in the boys an *esprit de corps*. Cleanliness is the A B C of self-respect, as self-respect is of respect for others; and here we do really "touch bottom."

As creepy, crawly, tickly creatures are brought by the boys from their houses to school, and as the Brahman thinks it wicked to take life, these interesting and lively little creatures have happy preserves on which to sport. Here is an incident I witnessed. A boy stood the tickling for some time, but at last his patience gave out; so he took the tickly one very carefully off his body, so as not to damage it. But what was he to do with it? If he put it on the floor, it would probably hop back to his own holy person. What he did was to put it in a place where it would be happy and contented, and that was a spot on a fellow-student's back, close to his neck, where the cover was plentiful.

Taffy's Kiss

That which makes one specially keen against this uncleanliness is that the Brahmans *will* call themselves "holy"; they cannot eat this, or touch that, for fear of defilement. So that when my clean, gentlemanly spaniel comes to school, and wishes to show himself friendly, the Brahmans one and all (except those who have learnt sense), draw their dirty persons and filthy clothes away from his clean coat for fear of pollution; and if by any chance this well-bred dog should touch them, a holy horror o'erspreads their faces. One day Taffy kissed a holy Brahman on the mouth. This was too awful. The boy was doomed to fast several days and, I believe, pay rupees to his family priest (who was probably many degrees dirtier than the wounded boy) before he could be pronounced clean.

Those Changing Eyes

Insolence and conceit, as well as "holiness" and dirty habits, are characteristic of the untrained Brahman youth. He cannot help them; they are hereditary, and he drinks them in daily, as he learns more and more of his superiority over mortals who are not the darlings of the gods. Only those who have *seen* that look in the eye can understand. It is a mixture of insolence, cunning, contempt, deceit, and conceit; if any one trait is stronger than the other I should say it is insolence.

Well! this look has to go out of the eye. And it is wonderful how quickly it does go: how and why, I don't quite know, but I think it is when they begin to learn to like and trust those whom they have been taught to despise. As these hateful barriers of caste prejudice are broken down, truth and light come into their souls and show themselves in the eyes.

It is one of the most interesting parts of our work to watch the eyes changing, for it means so much; it means growth and strength. Our men go to work at the eye with keenness, for they themselves had this disease once and know its cure.

When that characteristic look has gone, then you can begin to talk about manners; but until then the most useless thing in the world is talk.

The Weeping Parent

We can deal fairly effectively with the Kashmiri when we catch him young enough, while his character is still unformed and plastic. But the Brahman parent who has not been through the mill is a pretty hopeless case. The world holds no more precious piece of hypocrisy and conceit. Take this as an example of what he is capable of.

One fine day a man comes up to my house weeping, and says: "My son is dead!" I tell him that I'm sorry to hear it, and ask him the cause of death.

Weeping Parent: "He is not dead, but ready to die."

C. E. T.-B.: "Why, then, did you say he is dead when he is not?"

Weeping Parent: "Because he is so nearly dead, your master Bulla Kol having beaten him so hard with this stick."

(A huge thick stick, possibly with blood on it, is here produced.)

C. E. T.-B.: "Where is your son?"

Weeping Parent: "Here, sahib."

Enter one or two men carrying in a limp body, which is placed at the sahib's feet.

The pulse is felt and the patient examined, and after much trouble the clothes are removed in order to disclose the terrible wounds. The sore place happens to be on the fleshy part of the arm at the back, which, at the very first inspection, shows that the wale has been rubbed, scratched, and irritated in such a way as to appear severe.

I then draw the man on, saying : " What a terrible wound ! Do you mean to say that one of *my* masters inflicted such a wound ? " The weeping father, thinking that he has gained his point, grows bolder and says : " Yes, sahib, your master did this, and you must punish him very severely ; and if not, then I shall put the matter into the law courts."

I ask him if he himself has ever had a thrashing in his life, to which he replies in the negative.

" All the more pity, then. Get out of my sight at once, you scoundrel, or else you will now receive your long-deserved beating. Away with you and your 'dead' son ! And if your son returns to school and misbehaves himself, I will see that he is properly beaten before me."

The weeping father puts his tail between his legs and retires. And although he threatened to withdraw his son from the school at once, and prevent every one else from sending their sons to such a school, the dead son turns up at school alive and happy ; and, if I have laid it on sufficiently thick, the father also comes to beg pardon.

I write this at some length, as this is a common trick of the Kashmiri papa to punish an enemy. If you do not go hammer and tongs at this sort of game, you will probably land yourself and your masters in the law courts, as I did on one occasion ; but it has not happened again.

Kashmiri Psychology

Incidents like that which I have just related make

one think. Only, thinking does not help one to understand a Brahman. For that a Brahman's brains would be needed, a Brahman's traditions, and the queer angle from which this most oriental of Orientals views everything in heaven and earth. This "angle" is both obtuse and acute. It is an affliction that develops at quite an early age.

Why is it that when one speaks kindly to a boy and asks him to come to the mission school, he rarely comes, but if one tells him all about the dreadful things that will happen to him if he does come, such as having to learn about what he considers a false religion, having to play games *nolens volens*, punishments meted out handsomely and unsparingly, etc., he will probably come?

The query is answered by the following incident. I was speaking to a class about God's great love to us, and the reasons why we should return His love; and to drive the lesson home, and make it clear, I said: "Suppose in your school there were two masters of exactly opposite characters; the one hated the boys and was always hard on them, the other loved the boys and was always kind to them. Which of the two would you more readily obey?"

"The former," they all answered at once.

"Why?" I asked. "Because he would punish us if we did not."

I have found this to be perfectly true in other cases, though, of course, there are exceptions. If you wish a boy to stay at your school, do not be too kind to him, or visit him when he is ill or in trouble (though of course you do so, notwithstanding, knowing that right will prevail in the end), but be hard on him; and if you have occasion to punish him, then punish him severely, and he will love and follow you like a spaniel.

> A wife, a dog, and a walnut tree,
> The more you beat them, the better they be,
> But truer still of the Kashmīrī.

During our days of trouble, when friends were needed, this was most noticeable. The boys to whom we had been kind because of poverty or oppression, or for any other reason, were the very ones to leave us and jeer at us. Explain it how you will. I put it down to cowardice, which has become part of their nature, ingrained in them from their former years of oppression.

Conundrums

The questions we are asked are at times most amusing. Listen to the thought of Srinagar, transmitted to us by the boys.

The Chinese being the greatest people of the world, why do not they drive you sahibs out of India? This is a very common question.

The Sultan having defeated the *Sahib log* (English) in the Græco-Turkish war (for Greece, England, and all the European countries are one in their estimation), how do you expect to defeat the Afridis and other Mohammedans on the frontier?

How can Englishmen be in Ceylon, since Ceylon is the home of the gods?

Did you meet Babu Banerjee when you were in London, for he had gone there to finish his education?

Such are some of the wonderful conundrums that one has to solve; but with the help of the illustrated papers, backed up by geography and history, one is able to set the inquisitive minds on a straighter course. By the aid of the magic lantern, also, many an unintelligible problem and many a knotty question is easily explained, and the boys learn in the twinkling of an eye that which would take one many minutes to explain to one's own satisfaction while probably only further mystifying the questioner. Without a picture you have next to nothing from which to start.

"Funny" Sahibs

A former student of mine said to me: "You sahibs are funny people." "Why?" said I. "Because I have just seen on the notice board at the club the following:—'Found, a pearl brooch; the owner can have it by applying to——.'" I asked what was funny in that! "Why," said he, "we people would never do that, for if we find anything, we always believe that a god has put it there for us, and if we refused his gift it would make the god angry."

Before thieves start on a robbery, they always promise their god a percentage of the spoils, so that they may secure his help in their undertakings.

"I Was Worshipping"

If we could attain to the Kashmiri point of view, we Westerns would be more charitable. Obliqueness of vision accounts for much that, in our eyes, is moral obliquity. How else is their strange apathy towards people in distress to be accounted for? Let me give you an instance of this which fairly puzzled me. A certain young Brahman, a B.A. of the Punjab University, came to me as a witness at a life-saving case. He said that he was at the side of the canal doing his *puja*, i.e. worshipping his gods. A child fell into the canal a few yards away from where he was, when one of our teachers jumped in and saved the child. I asked him, if he saw the child drowning, why he did not go in himself and save it. He answered: "I was worshipping."

A *Shy* at "Dastur"

It is this sort of thing which we are up against continually. This is why we are so keen on social service. And considering the dead weight of custom that we have to fight, the progress made by our pupils is surprising. Why, many of them have learnt that *because* women are weak they should receive their protection and help, and we hear of kindly acts done by boys for their neighbours who are poor, and not for any pecuniary reward.

To those who live in Christian lands this will not seem to be anything out of the common, but such behaviour is extraordinary in this country. I trust that before long *dastur*, or custom, will have reached to this standard, if dastur must ever remain with us. I should like it to "go to Jericho," but if it did I expect all Kashmir would feel bound to follow it there. Education also had better "go to Jericho" if it cannot teach boys to live above dastur, to do a thing because it is right, and not because it is the custom.

Dastur has often tried to tie itself on to our boat, and more than that, tried to get in, but we have cut it off times out of number, and have ducked it, and held its head under water. But the beast won't die, any more than a locust; it is always appearing—"Here I am again." So we preach at it, we use it for a continual sermon, we put it up as a sort of Guy Fawkes or Aunt Sally, and throw volleys of abuse at it. Yes, dastur is a vile thing. It is something worth going for, and that is about the only good thing about it. But I hate dastur!

The River in Spate

Naturally, much of the social service to which we train our Srinagar lads has to do with the river on which the town stands. My readers would understand why I say "naturally," if they knew the Jhelum when it is in spate as well as in its normal flow. One flood I shall never forget. It literally burst upon us; for the city was dry at 11 a.m., and by 12.30 the houses were falling like ninepins in ten feet of water! It was hardly a time of peace and quiet, for all around the air was full of shrieks and yells as the poor inhabitants watched their houses coming down like packs of cards, sending the water and dust spouting up like a mine exploding. Over 2000 houses fell in the city, so there was no excuse for idleness. I will not bore you, but let me give you just an instance.

One of the junior teachers, a slightly built fellow, but a credit to his athletic training in the school, was attracted by the cries of many women, huddled together on a piece of dry ground which was fast growing less and less on account of the increasing waters. Close by were several boatmen in their boats, who were keeping an irritating distance and bargaining with those terrified women for an impossible salvage. The young master was naturally enraged at their brutality. Off went his coat, and the next second he was in the flood; before the astonished crowd could gasp he was in the boat, and out went the boatmen, but not before he had seized the paddle, with which he soon brought the boat to shore and rescued at his leisure the crowd of women; while the boatmen, robbed of their prize, vented their rage in their usual way, *à la* best Billingsgate, recounting the terrible things they would do to the young athlete when they got hold of him.

The Stumbling Block

The Brahmans have tried to make capital of this or that form of social service in which our boys engage and, although they know it is really for their own good, they pretend that it is a trick of the missionaries to out-caste their sons, and so to convert them to Christianity. We could have had several converts of this kind, had these been our ideas of Christianity; but no, conversion is something more difficult than this—it is nothing less than a complete change of hearts, not of customs or beliefs. The "holy" Brahman must learn that he is utterly filthy in God's sight like other men, that he has not one clean spot in him, and that he can only be cleansed by the blood of Christ. This is their stumbling-block, as it is of all men.

Outsiders do not often realize what it means for a Brahman to become a Christian. He will most certainly be an outcast from home, friends, and society, and must be ready to face possible death. When our young fellows tell us that they wish to become Christians, we always have to ask if they are willing to die for their faith. Some ask to be sent out of the country, but we do not believe in their running away.

A Mohammedan's *Story*

One of the Mohammedan boys, aged eighteen, a good all-round student and athlete, openly confessed his belief in Jesus as his Saviour. His father was naturally very much upset, and did all he could to dissuade him, first by promises of money, and a house, etc., and then, when this failed, the mullahs and fanatical Mohammedans obliged the father to employ threats. For many weeks the lad had a very severe time of persecution, which he bore bravely and cheerfully, for he possesses a very genial disposition. I visited his father, who is a really decent fellow, and told him that I was a father of boys and therefore could sympathize with him; that I should be very much upset if one of my sons gave up Christianity, but that I should be angry, not with my boy, but with the man who was the cause of my son's change of faith, if it were a matter of proselytizing. I pointed out that, if this change of religion on the part of his son were caused by me or by any other man's words, then he need not distress himself, for it would all come to naught; but that, if God Almighty had spoken to the boy's soul, then what could he or any one else do to prevent it? He quite accepted this view and was comforted, and gave his son leave to return to school.

But this happy state of things did not last, for the mullahs started again on the war-path, and the boy was beaten and driven from his home. This made the way clear for us to intervene. The doctors at the mission hospital very kindly made room for him, and we thought that perhaps he might now be left in peace. But this was not to be. We received news that a party of fanatics were lying in wait for him, to capture him on his road to or from school; so we put on an escort of school braves to guard him.

All went well until one day when the guards were ambushed outside the school, and a scuffle ensued as the guards held on to the lad's arms and the enemy to his legs. I do not know how the tug-of-war might have ended, had not Mr. Lucey, my colleague, appeared on the spot, when the battle went in our favour and the prize was landed safely in the school. The Mohammedans were by no means beaten, for a great mob surrounded the school compound and guarded most carefully every outlet. The school was closely invested for three hours.

Eventually Mr. Lucey was able to effect an escape by boat with the boy, his father, and the escort. The enemy then pursued in a boat, and tried to make a capture on the water, but there they were out-matched at once, as our men have not learnt aquatics for nothing. The enemy, finding that a water attack was useless, returned to dry land, and tried once more to attempt a rescue at the end of the water journey; but this also failed, and the boy was lodged once more in a friendly house. As we heard that the Mohammedans were determined to catch him, our only road out of the difficulty lay in sending him out of the country. He went to the Baring High School for Christian boys at Batala, where my brother was principal. There the boy was very happy.

The father behaved splendidly all the way through, and, if it had not been for the fanatics, would have treated his son well, as the latter was well over age and therefore able to choose for himself.

The Mohammedans have since turned their attention to their own schools, and have tried to persuade our Mohammedan teachers to leave us along with the Mohammedan boys, but so far without any success.

L'Envoi

The world of to-day isn't wholly as gay
As the Eden where Adam was placed ;

The thistles are rife in our corner of life
And half of the garden's a waste.

But it isn't discussing or staring or fussing
Will coax us a crop from the clay ;

It's draining, manuring, persisting, enduring,
It's patiently PEGGING AWAY.

Christ has Himself commanded us to go to all nations, to lead them to Him ; it is not easy, for the simple reason that it is like towing *up*-stream. God has committed to England a great empire, of which India is a part, and He has committed it unto us for a great purpose—not in order that we may simply grow rich, or for our own aggrandizement, but that we may give to India what we possess, namely, the Truth. God in His love has allowed us to know and accept Christ as our Saviour, and the least we can do is to pass on this knowledge to others. For it is not merely a belief, it is a life—a noble, unselfish life to be lived here, stretching into an eternal life beyond.

Therefore, if we are not destitute of human love, and if we have tasted anything of the power and riches of Christ, the least we can do is to pass on to others the knowledge of this eternal blessing.

Help us, then, give us a hand on the tow-line, to make these Kashmiri fellows under our charge true, manly, Christian gentlemen, as we tow up-stream to Him Who loved us and gave Himself for us.